my sister, my
confidante.
Love you,
Lora

RUNNING

UPHILL

A Memoir of Surviving Depressive Illness

or

"Still Crazy After All These Years"

Lora Inman

High-Pitched Hum
Publishing

© 2007 by Lora Inman

ISBN: 978-1-934666-09-8

Cover Design by Jennifer Wehrmann

Published and distributed by:
High-Pitched Hum Publishing
321 15th Street North
Jacksonville Beach, Florida 32250

Contact High-Pitched Hum Publishing at
www.highpitchedhum.net

For my husband Michael

and

My son Darin

With deepest love

In sooth I know not why I am so sad;
It wearies me; you say it wearies you.
But how I caught it, found it, or came by it,
What stuff 'tis made of, whereof it is born,
I am to learn.

--William Shakespeare
The Merchant of Venice (1600)

And now my life ebbs away;
Days of suffering grip me.
Night pierces my bones;
My gnawing pains never rest.

Job 30: 16-18

AUTHOR'S NOTE

Allowing for the obvious exceptions, a few of the names in this memoir have been changed to protect privacy. The events, however, remain true and unembellished.

RUNNING UPHILL

FOREWORD

It is with pride and honor that I write this foreword upon the request of the author, Mrs. Lora Inman. I feel fortunate to be part of one of Lora's triumphs on the completion of "Running Uphill." After reading the manuscript, I was quite overwhelmed with a gnawing sensation of pressure, and a bit of intimidation because I must give justice to the way the author presented her personal struggles with her disease. The apt description of the different phases of bipolar disorder is presented in a language that patients can relate to and empathize with. She walked us through her trials, troubles and triumph.

I join the millions who will undoubtedly applaud this book as the author narrated the episodes of "highs and lows" in different treatment options she tried; some with success and others with failures; her struggles and recovery.

Treatment is complex as the disease is affected by different variables, which include genetics, adverse life events, psychiatrists' experiences and inborn capabilities to genuinely care for their patients. More importantly, the treatment is heavily impacted by the lack of presence or absence of a healthy therapeutic relationship between the psychiatrist and the patient and the involvement with the family. The physiologic and pathologic changes in the brain and perhaps alterations in the brain's structure sometimes as a result of long-term treatment with certain medications are not fully understood. Some remain unknown and unpredictable at best. As complex as the brain is with all the "unknowns," together with other variables affecting presentation of each episode and thus response to treatment, the author shows her tenacity in beating this disease with increasing ferociousness with each episode. With periods of hopelessness and helplessness, there was a core spirit that fought to live.

When Lora first came to me stating she had been in treatment with a number of psychiatrists and therapists, the array of treatment available to man flashed across my mind. I repeatedly asked myself what, if any, could I offer her that has not been offered. The one thing I was sure of and was confident about at that point, was that Lora would not be alone. I would be with her through her depressed periods to make sure she did not forget her son, husband, friends, and other people who cared for her. Through her pleasant and unpleasant hypomanic and manic episodes, I was there to provide her mood stabilization through medications and counseling.

One particular visit stuck in my memory—from the waiting room she tried to hold back tears which became uncontrollable crying, and almost wailing as she gripped my arm so tightly I could feel her pain, which tore every fiber of my soul. For a long while I found myself speechless and all I could do was pray silently as I embraced her (something we are told as training residents never to do). As though by some process similar to osmosis I wanted desperately to absorb her pain, as I knew that once again the illness took away the strong person she is. I felt I should be stronger until her strength came back.

Lora's character and person, as I got to know her over the years, left an indelible imprint on my mind. The memory of a woman who struggled, yet somehow mustered all her courage to fight. She is one whose faith is unshakeable. She is real and honest about her transient vulnerability and perceived desperation, despite exhausting every new treatment. She attended various conferences and displayed a desire for continuing education. She always knew what was current in the treatment for bipolar disorder.

"Running Uphill" is a book that says it all. With all due respect to all who labored to come up with DSM IV with diligence and dedication, Lora Inman did an excellent job of offering anyone with the disease and their loved ones a down to earth and easily comprehensible presentation of the many ways by which the illness may present.

The challenge for anyone is immense. Unfortunately many have, for many reasons, failed to stay alive to experience the "life after the storm." It is difficult, but it can be done. Please reach out—there is help. Remember the most precious creation on earth is human life—YOU.

When the going gets rough, imagine your treatment team pushing you "uphill" when you seem to run out of steam.

This short contribution to Lora's great achievement allows me, on behalf of all psychiatrists, to thank all of our patients for the opportunity to be part of your recovery; for giving meaning to the career we, the physicians and psychiatrists, have labored to build. All of our efforts would have been in vain and worthless had it not been for your continued trust and confidence.

To NAMI and DBSA, more power and prayers as you persevere to put together seminars and support groups for those afflicted with this disease.

To the readers, may "Running Uphill" inspire you to increase your awareness to listen to your warning signs and red flags. Remind yourself of the importance of compliance to your treatment regimen. Most of all, may those of you with the illness always be enlightened by your spirituality, that after the "storm," the sun will shine again.

It is my hope, that in my own humble way of expressing my thoughts and feelings, I did justice to the efforts exerted by one of the most tenacious, sacrificing, and persevering (among many other attributes) persons I know, the author, Mrs. Lora Inman.

Emma B. Arellano-Cabusao, M.D.
Genesis Clinical Services
Chicago, Illinois

PROLOGUE

I wake up and look at the clock: 5:30 a.m. Thank God. I can stay in bed for another hour. I look at the clock every 5 minutes to see how much longer I can stay here. It's so safe here in bed. I can hide. I don't have to face anything. If I could just stay in bed, pull the covers over my head; and if it would just stay dark outside, then I wouldn't have to get up. I wouldn't have to feel guilty.

Finally it's 7:00 a.m. Now I'll really have to hurry to get to work on time. I don't want to get up. I don't want to get in the shower. I just want to stay here. But I force myself to get up and then I go get a cup of coffee. I shouldn't take the time; I should get right in the shower. At 7:15 I finally turn the water on and get in. Now I'm going to be late. Oh well, it's just a temp job. Nobody will notice. Am I getting depressed again? That's usually one of the warning signs: Not wanting to get out of bed.

No, lots of people don't want to get out of bed in the morning. It's ok. But I also notice I don't care as much about how I look or what I wear. It's been this way for the past week. Oh God, please, please don't let me get depressed again. I've felt really good for about a month now. But sometimes that's all I get—a month. Sometimes I get less than that. Then it comes back. No, I'll fight it. I'll just act as if I feel fine. I'm fine. I can't get depressed now! Mike's family is coming for a week. I can't function if I'm depressed.

Sometimes I'll sit here in the mornings and try to remember what it felt like when I wasn't depressed. I can remember times but I can't recapture feelings. The situation is the same. My life is the same. The circumstances are the same. But my perception of everything is distorted. I don't understand why my mood is black because of some chemicals floating around—or not floating around—correctly in my brain. It doesn't seem fair. It isn't fair. What scares me most is that sometimes I just feel like giving up. I don't want to, but what if I have to keep on going through these awful depressions for the rest of my life? What if I never find a solution or a treatment that works?

I've been tried on so many medications, even tried ECT when I was at my worst; and it still comes back. I hate what it does to me. I hate what it does to my family. I can't understand how a chemical imbalance could make such a difference in how I perceive the world. I hate "IT."

Conversely, when I'm feeling good—in between depressions—I can't remember the way it felt when I was depressed. Oh, I can remember that it was horrible; but it's almost as if it happened to someone else. During those "good" times, I really can't comprehend what could have possibly caused me to feel so hopeless. In between the depressions, I'm happy; I love my life, my husband, my son. I feel motivated, energetic, hopeful. I thank God for those times, and I keep praying they'll last. But they don't. For some unknown reason, I sink back into hell and I never know how long I'll be there before it goes away again.

I don't have the answers. I can only keep hoping to maintain the strength to get through those awful black, raging storms and remember that they have always passed although at the time it feels like it will go on forever and I'll never feel good again.

At least I've been able to force myself to go to work even when I don't feel like going. I need a reason to get up every day. I find that it's better than sitting at home wallowing in my misery, which only further aggravates the hopelessness I feel. For the time I'm at work, I can fake it well enough to make it through the days although inside I feel like shutting down completely. It's not an easy thing to push myself when I only feel like vegging out on the sofa in front of the television. If I want to survive, though, I have to make myself do things I don't really feel like doing.

Why can't people understand that no matter how much support you have from your loved ones, no matter how much they care about you and love you,

you are still completely alone with the feelings that seem more pervasive than anything else in your life.

I can't make anyone understand why I feel the way I do, or even express exactly what I feel, other than to tell them it's a sense of emptiness, of nothingness, of hopelessness, and a constant, nagging fear that it will never change, that I'll never again wake up with hope and love in my heart and with a desire to do things again other than stumble through the motions of living. How can I explain something that even I don't understand?

Much to my surprise, I have discovered that there are people who, even in this day and age, have never even heard of major depression, much less bipolar. Have they had their heads in the sand or what?

There are times when I'll be depressed for months; and sometimes Mike has to entertain some clients or go to some company function that requires my presence. I don't know how I actually do it, but for a few hours, I can manage to pull myself together and go to these functions without anyone ever knowing I really just want to die. I guess you could say I can be a fairly good actress when I need to be— but only for short periods of time. Having dinner is particularly difficult because I have no appetite. Food tastes like cardboard. Sometimes I'll just put it in my mouth and chew it and then spit it in my napkin when no one is looking, because I just can't swallow anything.

I'm so afraid that someone will find out how depressed I am and just run in the other direction. Why am I ashamed of something over which I have no control? What is it that causes some people to be so judgmental?

September 1994

Michael is out of town on business. Todd is gone somewhere for the night. I'm alone in the house.

Sometime after dark, I decide to go out to the garage looking for something to help me do this and notice the central vacuum hose in the corner. That might work. I cut off as much of the hose as possible and manage to get it haphazardly connected to the end of the tailpipe of my little red Acura. But when I try to put the other end into the car's front window, the hose pops off the tailpipe. Great. Looking around the garage for something to help, I spot a roll of duct tape. Taping the hose to the tailpipe is no easy task but I think it will hold.

Now that one end is taped, I try to put the other end into the front window but it won't quite reach. So I open the car's back door, roll the window down, pull some of the hose over the top into the car, and from the front seat, roll the back window up til the hose stays in place. Then I climb in through the front door, shut it, start the engine and climb into the back seat so I'll be closer to the hose. I sit back and wait. Fifteen or twenty minutes go by. Nothing. Nada. Not sleepy, not even drowsy. Still wide-awake and thinking this isn't going to work.

If I'd thought this through, made a plan, I would have taken some kind of tranquilizer to put me to sleep or at least make me drowsy, maybe even fortified the pills with a couple of stiff drinks. That would have been the smart thing to do if I was really serious about this. But unfortunately (or fortunately) I didn't plan ahead.

Depression does that sometimes. Keeps your brain from fully functioning. Thoughts are so random you have trouble formulating any kind of viable plan. You just react. You just want it to be over. You don't care how.

Finally, tired of sitting in the back seat waiting, I give up, crawl back over into the front seat, turn off the engine, get out of the car, pull the hose out the window and the other end off the tailpipe and throw it in the corner of the garage.

What else to do but use the little remaining energy I can muster to climb slowly up the stairs to the bedroom, and fall into bed, clothes still on, finally managing to fall into a troubled sleep.

The next day Mike comes home from his trip. I'm lying on the family room sofa watching taped reruns of "Friends" in my usual helpless stupor. He asks, "What the hell happened to the central vacuum hose?" "Oh, that. Well, I was going to kill myself last night but I got tired of waiting for the carbon monoxide to work and just gave up."

෨

There are a great many people who cannot remotely understand why someone would take their own life. They can't begin to imagine that kind of despair. When I hear people say really thoughtless, cruel things like, "How could anyone be so selfish as to kill themselves and leave everyone else behind to deal with it?" I want to scream at them, "They aren't selfish! People don't kill themselves out of selfishness or even because they really want to die." It happens because the pain of living in hell 24 hours a day is more than many in the midst of a devastating depression can continue to bear.

If you haven't been in this place, you cannot know. You cannot begin to understand. And you have no right to judge.

It's not that we don't want to live. It's that we don't want to live "like this." We feel a desperation and a hopelessness that most people can only imagine. I believe that depression carries with it an emotional pain that far exceeds any physical pain; and sometimes the only way to stop the agony is to completely give up.

Those of us who contemplate suicide know it's not rational. We know it will probably devastate those left behind and we hate ourselves for considering it. But when we can think of no way out, no other way to once and forever end the hell we perceive our lives to be, it seems like a reasonable option.

But the world doesn't accept death as an option. It asks us to continue to hang on and to continue to live, while the medical community continues to search for viable cures. We are prisoners of this malady, and our sentence is life. Nonetheless, in the absence of hope, we must keep struggling to survive—as many do—by the skin of our teeth.

The list of those who have taken their lives is long and tragic and a short list includes such well-known and creative people as Vincent Van Gogh, Abbie Hoffman, Virginia Woolf, Anne Sexton, Sylvia Plath, and Ernest Hemmingway. When you think of these tremendously creative men and women, you have to wonder what could cause a hopelessness so unbearable it would drive them to take their lives while others with similar symptoms manage to survive.

For those who have been fortunate enough not to have experienced what it's like to have severe, enduring, treatment-resistant depression, let me enlighten you with my own knowledge. All you experience is emotional pain with no possible cure. Feelings of complete isolation; unreasonable but terrifying fear; unrelenting hopelessness; apathy; lack of motivation and concentration; absence of pleasure; anger; agitation; paranoia; undue sensitivity to criticism; loss of self-esteem; thoughts that life is not worth living. Imagine living with these feelings for weeks, months, or even years while you're switched from one medication to another, some of them even intensifying the very feelings you're trying to alleviate.

I'm not talking about the kind of depression that everyone feels at one time or another, the kind you feel because of something that happens in your life. It's normal to feel depressed when someone you love dies, when your husband or wife leaves you, when you're failing in school. Many people know what it's like to be "down-in-the-dumps" but not to be "paralyzed." Major depression is something beyond unhappiness. It's a full-scale fall into an abyss.

I've learned that while our individual stories differ, those of us who live with depressive illness share a common bond. We struggle to survive, to climb out of the emotional hell that depression is, to find a solution and to dream of a cure that we must believe is just over the horizon. Those of us who've fought this battle not just once, but over and over, hang on tenaciously to the promise of a cure that we must believe is just around the corner—a hope that for many of us is the only reason we continue to live.

My experience with depression and ultimately bipolar disorder (manic depression) has shaped my world in ways I'll probably never fully understand. It has affected my relationships, my career, and my family. At times it has been like an evil force, a relentless and unpredictable enemy, disappearing for weeks or months, then returning with a vengeance.

December 20, 1996

It's five days til Christmas. I'm once again in the pit of hell. I'm 50 years old. I've been battling this crap for over 25 years. I'm not weak. No one who is weak would have survived this long. I'm scared. I'm angry. I'm hopeless. I'm tired. I'm ready to give up. But I can't.

I don't blame this on God; I just wish I could understand why I continue to suffer. I hate this! I haven't had to live with cancer or heart disease or MS or a million other horrible illnesses so I can't say mine is worse. But for me, there is nothing that could compare to this emotional hell. No one can make it go away, no one can make it better. There is no magic pill and no one can wave a magic wand or rearrange my entire brain chemistry so I no longer have to live with it. In fact, no one knows for sure what even causes it to happen to some people and not others in the first place. This has nothing to do with anything anyone ever did or did not do to me or for me. I've fought so hard and so long, always trying to convince myself that there really is hope, that somewhere out there if I can just hold on long enough, there will be a cure. I've been told this illness has made me a stronger person. It probably has. I just don't think I can stand to get any stronger.

November 18, 2000

It comes from out of nowhere, obliterating previous thoughts and feelings, destroying all that was before, changing me into an anomaly no longer recognizable even to myself. It's tentacles spread themselves like a cancer through my body into my brain, feeding on the life that was once there and leaving behind a frightened, desperate shell of a human who crawls through each day certain that this time it will not leave as it has always done in the past but this time will stay and complete it's task.

The days are endless, without color or hue, much like a gray day of winter when the trees are in death, leaves long gone. Hope of spring, of rebirth, is never to be felt again. In nature, seasons come and go and spring follows winter when the ice thaws and buds spring up again and blossom; and the cycle of life once again becomes beautiful. Not so with the demon of depression. The trees remain in death eternally— immobile, unmoving, and accepting only of the icy coldness that comes with winter. There will never again be a spring or a summer or even a fall. There is no hope. Hope is a word that never was. Michael reminds me of hope, promising me I have been in this place before and it has always ended and it will again. But this time it will not leave as it has always done in the past. This time it will stay and complete its task.

There have been so many winters before that have ended and life has returned to me. But this one I will not make it through. I'm too weak from hanging on. I have the strength of one whose body has been ravaged by cancer so badly that death would be a kind ending to the sufferer. But for me, it is my mind that has been ravaged by the depression, so completely stripped of any remote form of hope that death would be a welcome ending to the enormous emotional pain of having my mind consumed with black and tortured thoughts and feelings.

I have stayed alive for my son. How could a child, even a grown child, understand a mother who would take her own life? How would he learn to accept it, even knowing that I've had this illness for years? Could he ever understand that for me, it was only an end to the pain that I desired? Could he ever believe that if I truly loved him as I do that I could leave him without a mother? And worse still, what if by some awful chance he developed the disease himself and was left alone without me there to carry him through it as only one who has been there before could? He is so proud of my tenacity and my strength. How could I take that from him?

Then suddenly, for no apparent reason, I wake up one day, months after this demon has inhabited me, and I think I might feel like getting dressed and leaving the house. But I'm afraid to trust the feeling. So I tell no one. I simply continue to wait. And then the next day I wake up and it's gone. Completely. As if the prayers for me have at last been heard by God and He has answered. I am grateful beyond explanation but I do not understand.

This is the story of my own personal struggle with depression and ultimately bipolar disorder. Most of my adult life has been an uphill struggle to survive countless episodes of major depression. Years of my life have been lost while I numbly moved around in a gray fog waiting for the depression to end.

I believe I have suffered from dysthymia (a chronic but less severe form of depression characterized by moods that are consistently low, but not as extreme as major depression) since my early 20's. According to the DSM-IV, the psychiatric manual used by mental health professionals in diagnosing mental disorders, those who experience dysthymia are more likely to develop subsequent major depression.

Major depressive disorder, dysthymia, and manic depression are considered types of a clinical depression because they are biologically based illnesses triggered by chemicals in the brain. Situational or reactive depression, on the other hand, is triggered by distressing life events such as the death of a loved one, rather than by biological causes. However, if situational or reactive depression increases in intensity, or lasts for more than two weeks, it can evolve into clinical depression.[1]

Throughout this memoir, the term "depression" is used to mean major or clinical depression.

Depression affects some differently. A few people are able to get up and function almost normally in the mornings but as the day progresses, the mood worsens and a sense of dread and anxiety slowly creeps in. But my situation was just the opposite. It's impossible to describe the long stretches of time when I'd awake in the morning with this paralyzing fear of something I couldn't even name, and then count the hours that had to pass before I could crawl back into bed and escape for awhile into sleep, all the while knowing that morning would come again and bring with it the agony of crawling through yet another day without relief. Nighttime for me was less difficult than the mornings, maybe because I was comforted by the thought that at night I could at least sleep for several hours—shut my brain off temporarily.

Depression steals away whoever you were, prevents you from believing in a future, and replaces your life with a black pit. Nothing human beings value matters any more—music, laughter, food, love, sex, vacations, work—because nothing and no one can reach the person trapped in the void.

You don't understand why you no longer want to live. You don't understand why all the things you once loved so completely no longer matter. You don't understand why the home you once spent time so lovingly decorating has now become nothing more than a place in which you can hide from the world outside. You wonder how the ravenous appetite you once had for food is replaced by complete disinterest in eating at all, how reading a book was something you once loved. You never know what will happen next or when it might be over or even if it ever will.

In the last 8 to 10 years, there have evolved a myriad of advertisements for medication meant to alleviate depression. There's currently one on TV showing a little "neurotransmitter" looking sad and down. And the ads suggest that if you're feeling any of the symptoms I've already mentioned, you just might be able to take this little pill and life will be just swell again. Been there, done that, got the t-shirt.

The estimated 20 million people suffering from depression are victims of an illness over which they have no control. And although media studies often claim that a cure is just around the corner, we've come to discover that drugs like Prozac, although it has done wonderful things for many people, is clearly not the panacea for the millions who hoped it would be.

This may seem an anomaly, but over the years I've developed a very dry—maybe even warped—sense of humor and invariably make a joke of my pain. If I let despair overcome me, I'll sink into self-pity so deep that I can't crawl out. It's necessary for me to find humor in the tragic in order to survive. You may think me callous for seeking laughter in loss, and I'll admit to having been hopeless in many respects, but as long as I can laugh, I'm not without hope. I can refer to myself at times as "crazy" or "wacko" to take the edge off the pain. I used to tell Mike that being married to me was like having two different women because he'll never know which Lora he'll wake up with. "Crazy Woman" is something he affectionately calls me, which may seem awful to some, but if we both can find some way to laugh at all the absurdity—if I'm able even to laugh at myself—it doesn't seem as bad as it could otherwise.

Although there's absolutely nothing funny about depression, or suicide, there are moments, even in the sea of pain, that humor provides a life raft.

∽

I don't remember a great deal about my early childhood. I didn't exactly grow up in the Beaver Cleaver family. I never really knew my father, don't recall ever having a conversation with him. My parents were divorced before I was born. At least that's what I was told; I don't know the details. Even now, some 50 years after the fact, I know relatively little about my biological father *or* my mother's relationship with him. Based on the few pictures of him I have, and what little I remember of seeing him the few times I did as a child, I remember him as a sternly handsome man of medium height. I don't recall ever hearing him laugh or seeing him smile.

I do know that the absence of a father's love in my life has had a profound influence in my relationships with men. This is a common thread among many women who grow up without a father: A desperate need for approval, a search for someone to fill the emptiness in our souls, to give us the love that was denied, to make us whole.

For years I had unresolved ambivalence about my father. How much did he really care about me? Maybe it would have been better to go on the accumulated evidence of absenteeism and benign neglect and admit that there was no profound connection. Maybe if you really believe that there is no parental love at all, you don't spend any time searching for it, either in your parents or in surrogate and successive sexual partners. You don't keep trying to please them, to live off the crumbs of praise or approval that you can then falsely interpret as proof of their affection for you, their esteem. If you don't know the full truth about what either of your parents thought of you, if you can't really know what went on inside their heads, then you can't know anything for sure about other people who are even less close to you.

After more than 30 years, just two years ago, I decided to fly to Little Rock to visit my cousin Ruth (my mother's first cousin); and maybe embrace some of my past, see where my mother grew up, get to know something about my roots. It was a beautiful time of the year and the day after I arrived at Ruth and Joe's, she asked if I might want to visit some cemeteries where many of my ancestors were buried. I wanted to.

A kind, easygoing, and loving person, Ruth is the only close family member with whom I've kept in touch with over the years, and about the only person who's ever shared any of my family history with me. She's also the one person I trusted enough to call several years ago to ask if there might possibly be some genetic link in our family that could provide some clue as to why I was cursed with depression. I

influence in my life; that he remarried and moved on; I doubt he ever looked back.

My half sister was born when I was six. Sadly, with the age difference, we never became close. I regret that. I mostly regret not being there for her in later years when she so needed me. Eventually the trauma she experienced throughout her own child-hood and even as a young adult would cause her to take her own life at the age of 39, leaving behind a young son emotionally damaged by the loss of his mother. Depression is a gift that keeps on giving.

My grandma lived with us for a while and I remember mother and her shouting at each other sometimes. I recall mother telling her she hoped she never treated her own daughters the way her mother treated her. I'm still not sure what it was all about and I can't even say why I remember this. I remember grandma with thinning white hair that was always coiled in a bun at the back of her head, something I sometimes did for her. Like my father, though there was no biological connection, I have no memory of hearing her laugh or seeing her smile. There simply didn't seem, at least in my own memory, much emotion in our family, or much expression of love.

It was the silence and emptiness of our home that disturbed me most. There was precious little joy or laughter. There was so much silence. Always the silence. I wasn't allowed to play the radio—listen to the popular music all my friends listened to—even when getting ready for school. I recall a morning when I was in the kitchen fixing my lunch for school; and I turned on the radio, really, really low. Mother hollered at me from the living room, "Turn that noise off." Neither my sister nor I, for the most part, was allowed to play the radio or watch TV because when mother wasn't teaching school she was immersed in reading *Science and Health with Key to the Scriptures* by Mary Baker Eddy, the founder of the Christian Science religion. She was fanatical about Christian Science, a religion drilled into her by my grandma from the time she was quite young.

During a conversation a few years ago, my cousin Ruth said to me, "Your mother was a very bright young woman and had a good heart." When discussing my mother's fanatical religious beliefs, Ruth said, "Your poor mother never stood a chance. She was brainwashed from day one. Her own mother was never nurturing. She was too consumed with reading her religious literature to pay much attention to her daughter, or her two sons."

In hindsight, I've asked myself if my mother unwittingly and unknowingly did the same in the treatment of her own children, not understanding the damage done to her and not knowing how to stop passing the dysfunction on to the next generation.

Christian Science taught her to believe nothing that her five senses told her. She believed, or *tried* to believe, that the only world that truly existed was a world where there *was* no sin, sickness, or death. They were simply false beliefs conceived by "mortal mind." Quoting from *Science and Health*, page 229, Mrs. Eddy states: "It is the transgression of a belief of mortal mind, not of a law of matter nor of divine Mind, which causes the *belief* of sickness. The remedy is Truth, not matter—the truth that disease is unreal." Sounds pretty clear, right?

That was the problem I always found with this Mary Baker Eddy. Most of what she wrote was ambiguous at best; and even later on when I tried to read some of her writings in an attempt to understand why it was my mother was so fervent about Christian Science, it still made very little sense, just a bunch of pseudo-intellectual jargon thrown together in some obscure order to entice her readers into believing she could heal them without doctors or medicine. But I'll give her one thing: She did make a lot of money at it.

This was the world my mother tried to embrace; one she desperately tried to believe was perfect. A pretty radical concept to hold onto when her oldest daughter was growing a tumor on one ovary which would later turn out to be the size of a watermelon and weigh 19 pounds. Years later, when I asked how she could possibly deny that a 19 pound cyst was removed from my body, her reply was, "Well, to human sense it *seemed* real." *It seemed real? Give me a break. Trust me, I had the surgery. It was real.*

Anytime I was sick she admonished me not to believe my senses, but to *deny* it; and that if I did so strongly enough, the symptoms would simply disappear. It was all about mind over matter. I think it was the only way she could survive: by living in denial. Looking back, I feel badly for her; her entire life was based on fantasy, and still she was not a happy person throughout most of it.

About the time I was beginning puberty, I was sexually molested. I never told anyone. Why? Why does any child endure molestation? There are many reasons: Because they are afraid to tell; perhaps no one will believe them; maybe they'll be blamed somehow. I was a child, for God's sake. I was vulnerable. I didn't *know*. But I know now that it does irreparable damage to the victim's sense of self, affects their self-esteem for the rest of their lives, leaves emotional scars. I wasn't able to tell anyone about it until my early twenties when I first started experiencing depression. Even then it was humiliating to reveal, even to a psychiatrist, that it happened, because somehow it still felt like my fault. Those things just didn't happen to "normal" people, so obviously, I must not be normal.

❦

In 1960, my mother, my stepfather, my half-sister, and I were living in California. Mother taught school. We didn't have a lot of money. I never got new clothes for school every year like most of my friends. We never went hungry but we had less than most of the other families I knew. I can remember meals of fried Spam, fried bologna, and sardines in a can. A real treat for me was coming home from school before anyone else was home, taking chocolate cocoa from the cupboard and mixing it in a pan with sugar and margarine til it was hot and melted together; then I'd just eat it with a spoon. It was heaven.

Sometime the next year, my mother and step-father divorced. Now on top of everything else I was not only living in a dysfunctional family but also in a single-parent family at a time when few other people were.

I felt, in so many ways, "different." I was terrified that people might find out things about my family that I was so ashamed of. How could I possibly have developed any degree of self-esteem?

I was painfully shy throughout grade school, not one of the popular, outgoing kids; a gangly little girl with freckles and a slightly crooked smile. My freshman year of high school was a sort of coming out for me. I made new friends and discovered that boys thought I was pretty and began to notice me.

I still wanted to hide my family life. I never had girlfriends over to spend the night, didn't want anyone to see how we lived. I did most of the household chores and even a lot of the cooking because mother was constantly studying her religious propaganda. I didn't want anyone to think my mother was strange because it was a reflection on *me*. I didn't want anyone to know we weren't a *normal* family.

I recall an instance when I was outside hanging clothes on the line and later overheard a neighbor tell another neighbor, "That poor girl does all the work while her mother sits around and reads her Bible." I was horribly ashamed. I desperately wanted to be in a normal family like everyone else. I was so afraid of what the neighbors thought of my mother that when I did have to do chores outside—like watering the plants or hanging clothes on the line—I tried to do it only when I didn't think anyone could see me.

Mother was never intentionally mean or cruel; she was simply trying to survive a life that had never been easy for her. She wasn't raised in a normal family; how could she know what one actually was? I know now she did the best she knew how at the time. She wanted her two daughters to embrace her religion of avoidance as she did. For whatever reasons, she wasn't able to face the reality of how things really were. I know my mother loved me but nowhere in my memory bank do I remember her telling me so, not in my childhood years anyway.

Near the end of my freshman year of high school, mother told me that she, my sister, and I were moving to Arkansas, which was where my biological father lived. I'm reasonably sure her decision was based on the hope they would get back together. It never happened.

Suddenly, whatever newfound acceptance and security I was just beginning to feel among my peers was to be taken away as remarkably as it had come.

I started 10th grade in Arkansas, a sharp contrast in comparison to life in California. This was the south in the 60s. We're talking segregated schools and a time when blacks weren't considered as equals. Governor Faubus was attempting to integrate Central High School in Little Rock. Chaos was everywhere. To avoid the integration situation, I was enrolled in a small segregated high school in a neighboring community.

One of my good friends in my freshman year in California was a black man, president of the student body, and a person I liked and admired. This new location was going to be vastly different from what I had come to know and expect. I was a newcomer and a stranger among kids who'd grown up together in a completely polar environment. I was still shy and unsure of myself at an age when hormones are going through incredible changes in the process of growing from a child into a young woman. It was a time when self-image was of paramount importance in attempting to make new friends and fit into a place completely foreign from what I'd known.

And then, to add insult to injury, another catastrophic event began to manifest itself: I became aware that my stomach stuck out more than normal. I was a skinny kid anyway so I couldn't understand why I was developing a large stomach instead of the flat stomachs seen on the other girls my age.

It got worse. My stomach got bigger. I managed to hide it for the most part by wearing loose-fitting clothes; but it was a traumatizing experience to go through what should have been my happiest years thinking I was deformed and knowing I was "different" from the other girls my age, not only because of my family situation but also physically. We didn't, of course, go to doctors for religious reasons thus I was condemned to living out my high school years in ignorance of what was wrong with me, trying desperately to look like everyone else; trying even harder to hide the fact that I didn't. I wouldn't even go swimming with a group because I'd have to wear a bathing suit and then everyone could see there was something wrong with me.

What more could life dump on me? This physical disfiguration had a devastating impact on how I viewed myself; and the fact that I didn't even know what it was only added to my shame. In my own eyes, I was a freak—one more thing that could be added to the ever-growing list of reasons I just might not reach adulthood as the brightest bulb in the socket.

I graduated from high school, married my high school boyfriend—who, for reasons still unknown, didn't seem to notice I was "deformed"—and we moved to Kansas. We were only kids—17 and 18 years old. Immature would be an understatement. What possessed me to get married at such a ridiculously young age?

I wanted to get away from home, away from what I considered my increasingly dysfunctional and pitiful family; and in my desperate need for love combined with my already low self-esteem, I thought it was the best I could hope for. Here I was, physically deformed (at least in my own eyes), not allowed to see a doctor, living in an environment I despised, and there was this one person who actually wanted to marry me. What was I thinking? I'd never had a real childhood, never had a chance to define my identity, to figure out just who I really was. I was devoid of any real maturity. I jumped from the frying pan into the fire.

It turned out to be an emotionally and physically abusive relationship; but there was one upshot. Now that I no longer lived with my mother, I could finally make the choice to seek medical attention and find out what gross deformity I might have.

For the first time in my life I made an appointment to see a doctor. Ashamed to let him see my body, afraid of what awful thing I might have and fearing that nothing could be done, I reluctantly confessed that I thought I was deformed and allowed him to look at my stomach. After a short exam, he told me he thought I had a tumor or a cyst, probably about the size of a grapefruit. But the good news was that it could be removed.

Some tests were done, surgery was scheduled and the surgeon opened me up and removed a 19-pound ovarian cyst from my right ovary. I was told it had to have been growing for at least 6 years or more to reach that size. This was 1964. The medical technology we now have was not yet available. We didn't have Ultrasound, CAT Scans, or MRIs. Surgeons pretty much didn't know what they'd find before they opened you up.

I left the hospital with a 12-inch scar down the middle of my stomach. At least I wasn't carrying around a 19-pound tumor any longer; and I could actually start wearing normal clothing. It was almost like being born again. The hospital even gave me a color slide of the cyst because it was a record for the hospital. I used to carry the slide in my wallet—God only knows why—but somewhere along the way I lost it.

I was relieved to know what had been wrong with me and glad to be rid of it; nonetheless a part of me was angry with my mother that I'd had to endure this disfiguration all through my teen years. And she was angry with me for not trusting God to heal me—actually resorting to medical treatment instead. Can you believe this?

Years later, my cousin Ruth shared with me what my mother said to her following my surgery: "It's her own damn fault for believing a lie." *Having the surgery was my fault because of my own misguided belief that the cyst was a reality?*

It's important to acknowledge that while I was growing up, anytime I was sick my mother admonished me not to believe my senses, but to *deny* it; and if I did so strongly enough, the symptoms would simply disappear. It was all about mind over matter; I think it was the only way she could survive. In retrospect, my heart breaks for her. Her whole life was based on denial. She desperately needed to believe that God was in complete control; therefore nothing bad really existed. Still, unhappiness seemed to pursue her.

‿

The physical abuse in my marriage continued. The night I came home from the hospital from my surgery, he demanded sex. Oh, there was no saying, "No." He wanted what he wanted and he didn't care about anything else. Basically he raped me. Is it any wonder I wanted out? I was afraid of him but what could I do? I had no place to go. I couldn't go home, couldn't possibly go back to that. I didn't think I could support myself. I'd never even had a job of any kind—not in high school—not ever.

About four years into the marriage, a miracle happened: Uncle Sam intervened. My husband was drafted. It wasn't that I wished him to have to go in the Army, but the fact that doing so would end the abuse was a positive. After he left for basic training, I began to realize there was a real possibility that I just might be able to take care of myself and didn't have to take the abuse I was used to. However, even then I didn't just throw in the towel without trying to salvage my marriage. At one point, I even quit the job I'd gotten and moved to live with him near the Army based where he was in basic training. Still the abuse continued. I made the decision to move back to Kansas, got my old job back, and eventually filed for divorce.

For the first time in my life I was truly alone. And I functioned. I had a job. I got a roommate. I got a life. Well, at least I tried. It was a start. I was 20 years old. The major depressions hadn't yet hit but all the pieces from the past were already in place. You take someone with already low self-esteem, put them in an abusive relationship, throw in a chemical imbalance and it's a major depression waiting to happen.

I don't mean to infer that having a rotten childhood or going through major trauma in one's life causes major depression. There are many who have had terrible childhoods and yet never experience it. Conversely there are also those who come from warm, loving, supportive backgrounds who still experience major depression or bipolar disorder. Over the years I've spent literally thousands of dollars on psychologists, psychiatrists, social workers—all kinds of mental health professionals—digging into my past thinking that my problems, my mood swings, were somehow connected.

The years following my divorce were an important yet difficult period. No one had ever taught me I had any value. I was just a "dumb kid." I grew up in a family that didn't exactly meet the criteria of functional, and my most formative years were filled with a belief that I was a freak. Even if no one else could see it, I could. I wasn't even allowed to find out why. I was continually told that I looked the way

I did because I didn't "deny" it strongly enough. If I didn't get better, or well, or look normal, it was my own fault for my lack of faith.

And then the first and only man in my life who had purported to love me treated me as someone put on earth to meet *his* needs. He certainly didn't *respect* me. How could I have developed any confidence in myself? Things like that take a long time to unlearn.

I think it was Groucho Marx who said, "I wouldn't want to belong to any club that would have me as a member." I embraced that philosophy. It fit. Why would anyone with any real value want to be with me? Only someone who had something wrong with them also would want me; and I certainly didn't want to be with someone who had something wrong with them. I think they call that a "catch 22."

Had I been able to work through that negative self-imagine, there was one relationship during those early years following my divorce that might have evolved into a life-long commitment. But I wasn't yet in that place. I still had demons to deal with, still needed to define exactly who I was, what I was capable of, and what I deserved. Why did it take me so long to get there?

I felt generally "down" much of the time through that period. Not the major depressions that came later, but the dysphoria I mentioned earlier (although

I'd never even heard of the term "dysphoria" until I read the DSM-IV years later).

In the late '60's and early '70's, most people, myself included, had never even heard of disorders called depression or manic depression. The term bipolar disorder, a newer term for manic depression, hadn't even been adopted yet. If such disorders existed, no one I knew had ever heard of them. Many psychiatrists in the 1970's still considered depression purely psychological, the consequence of some nonsensical cause such as gender identity or faulty potty training. (Even more frightening, a few psychiatrists still subscribe to that hypothesis.)

Because these "down periods" seemed to go on and on, I finally made an appointment with a psychiatrist in the hope that I could find out what was wrong with me. He wasn't much help. He didn't offer any chemical imbalance possibilities or provide any explanation as to why I would fall into these dark periods of despair. I don't remember exactly what he said—it was over 40 years ago—but I do know I walked out of his office not one bit wiser nor with any hope of getting better. I had absolutely no clue that this was partly a physical illness. I didn't even know it *was* an illness. At that time I'd never even heard of a chemical imbalance, didn't know it could be treated with antidepressants, hadn't even heard of antidepressants; antidepressants weren't in anyone's vocabulary I knew of. And this psychiatrist didn't even mention them.

I'll never know what "caused" my depression. As much as I currently know, no one has a precise answer as to what actually causes depression in anyone. To be able to do so will likely prove to be impossible because the intermingled factors of abnormal chemistry, behavior, and genetics are too complex. Probably multiple components are involved, in fathomless combinations.

As I got older, these episodes of dysphoria became more frequent and more severe, and try as I might to find out why and what I could do about it, I wasn't very successful; but I never stopped searching for answers. I read everything I could find about depression. Unfortunately, in those years, there was precious little to be found. We didn't have computers in those days; you couldn't just "google" depression on the Internet. Short of Sigmund Freud's works, and Sylvia Plath's *The Bell Jar* (a real upper, let me tell you), I could find nothing about depressive illness. Let me warn you: If you're feeling depressed, *The Bell Jar* would not be a book I'd recommend.

Over the last 30 years, there has been a cornucopia of medications I have tried that have failed, not to mention the homeopathy, herbal remedies, changes in diet, acupuncture, sleep deprivation, counseling, yoga, faith healers—you name it. What God would allow a person to suffer like this?

And then came the inevitable: electroconvulsive therapy (ECT), once known as shock treatments. After seeing *One Flew over the Cuckoo's Nest*, ECT wasn't my treatment of choice. But as a person with treatment-resistant depression, I relented to this treatment as a last resort. I was *determined* to find, if not a cure, then *something* that would help lessen the severity of these depressions and give me a reason to hang on.

When depression finally "came out of the closet" when at last I discovered that others had experienced these horrible mood swings, that I wasn't singled out as I'd originally believed, I didn't feel quite so alone. I've since learned that many creative and famous people have experienced major depression or manic depression.

Abraham Lincoln, Isaac Newton, Chopin, Mozart, Beethoven, Charles Dickens, Winston Churchill, and Mark Twain are only a few comprising a very long list. A more recent list includes such people as Dick Cavett, Rod Steiger, Patty Duke, William Styron, Thomas Eagleton and Mike Wallace.[2]   Some have shared their stories with the public, which has helped to lessen, but not completely alleviate, the stigma associated with what most people perceive as a "mental illness."

Prior to sometime in the 19th century, admitting you suffered from severe depression was tantamount to being declared insane and locked up in some psychiatric hospital. I recall reading the book *Shadowland*[3] about the actress Frances Farmer (1913-1970) and her commitment to Steilacoom Hospital in Washington State. Pretty scary stuff. A claim made in an article by the Citizen's Committee on Human Rights states:

> *Frances Farmer was a successful screen and stage actress in Hollywood and Broadway in the 1930s and 1940s. Jessica Lange later portrayed her story in the movie, Frances. Upset over a string of failed relationships, Farmer was involuntarily committed in 1943. For seven years, she was subjected to 90 insulin shocks and electroshocks, and was sold by psychiatric workers to drunken sailors who repeatedly raped her. She told of being "raped by orderlies, gnawed on by rats, poisoned by tainted food, chained in padded cells, strapped in strait jackets and half drowned in ice baths. Her last "treatment" was a lobotomy by Walter Freeman. Farmer never regained her abilities and died, destitute.[4]*

Although I've discovered that some of what was written about her is fiction, it's still not a pretty picture. Thank God we've progressed since then.

I don't think anyone who has experienced depression has experienced the exact, identical thoughts and feelings. We're all different after all. We each have our own demons, our own memories, our own terrors and fears that are peculiar only to ourselves. There seems to be commonness, however, in that those in the midst of a depression feel frighteningly alone and shut off from the rest of the world.

And to make it even worse, those of us with depressive illness get to hear someone like Tom Cruise espouse on national television, "There is no such thing as a chemical imbalance," suggesting that major depression is caused by some innate weakness in ourselves that we're just not strong enough or smart enough to see past.

I wouldn't wish this illness on anyone. I can, however, think of one or two people whom I'd like to see experience it for a while. Maybe then they'd get a sense of it. How can anyone actually believe we can just "think ourselves" out of real major depression by positive affirmations? Amazingly, some do.

Major depression is a dark, terrifying place to find oneself in. I've been there many times. Thousands of others have also. Sitting in the waiting room of my psychiatrist's office, I've seen some of them. I've seen their pain. I recognize it. I've identified with the terror in their eyes, the hopelessness etched in their faces. Many times I've wanted to lean over and say, "I understand. I've been where you are. Don't give up."

It is an insidious gloom that takes over your brain without you even being able to recognize what's happening. When you are "in it" there is no more empathy, no intellect, no imagination, no humanity, no hope. Depression steals away whoever you were, prevents you from believing in a future, and replaces your life with a black pit.

You have vague memories of who you were before, but no matter how desperately you try to remember that time—to recapture that desire to live—you can't grasp it. It's a distant memory of something good, something that you were *before*. Something you fear you will never be again. Nothing matters except ending the pain. Suicide sounds like the only solution but you torture yourself with thoughts of how it would affect your children, your parents, your spouse. How can you destroy their lives too?

Although there is currently no cure for depression, it is estimated that approximately 80% of those who will experience clinical depression have available to them a myriad of antidepressants which will alleviate their symptoms and allow them to live normal lives. But one can't help but think of the 20% of those millions with depressive illness for whom these drugs don't bring relief. For many years I fit into that category, and I was not alone. There are still approximately 3.5 million others. And the more frequently the depressions come, the longer they last, the more treatments you try that don't bring relief, the more your resolve is depleted, the more hopeless you feel, and the closer you come to simply giving up. Where do we turn? Who wants to continue to live with an illness which immobilizes you so completely that merely to function in the day-to-day events that are part of life involves an effort carrying with it an emotional pain so devastating that you can't imagine being able to survive one more day? How do you make someone who knows nothing about depression understand why you are unable to function, why life is, in *your* mind, so utterly hopeless that you need help of a kind even you don't understand? You can't. You have to have felt it yourself.

A year or so ago I was having a conversation with my now adult son about my depression. I shared the "garage episode" story with him. We laughed at the absurdity of it. I said, "I guess I just wasn't meant to die so soon." He told me, "I'm glad, because if you had killed yourself, I probably would have killed myself, too."

Please, please think of those words if you're ever tempted to take your own life. More than anyone, a child cannot possibly understand why his parent would take his or her own life. They ask themselves questions like, "Was it my fault?" "Did my mother not love me enough to stay alive?" "What did I do to make my dad leave me?" It's a terrible burden to place on a child. A child who loses a parent to suicide is scarred for life.

In a paralyzing grip of a depressive episode, many times I would say to myself, "If I can just hang on for one more day, it might go away. It always has in the past. It will again." So I would wait. For days. Weeks. Sometimes months. If you're lucky, it goes into remission. Your hope comes back. You begin to enjoy things again; look forward to doing things you haven't felt like doing forever. The light comes on, pushing the darkness into the background. Once more, you feel hope. You start to feel like you just might want to continue living. You tell yourself that maybe it's over for good. Maybe this will be the last time you'll have to go through this awful nothingness. Maybe you can get on with your life.

❧

Sometime in 1977 the company I was working for was moving its headquarters to Nevada and I was asked to move with them. I'd never moved anywhere on my own but I decided to go. I wasn't exactly living in bliss where I was so what did I have to lose?

Immediately after my move, I rented an apartment and was in the process of moving in when I was hit with a depression that knocked me completely off my feet. It was the first major depression of many to come later. I'd been depressed, but not this terrifying kind of panic I was feeling now. It wasn't like something bad had happened to cause it. For no reason I could comprehend, I suddenly felt like life was no longer worthwhile and I didn't even know why. It was as if I was suddenly thrown into a world in which no one else lived. I could barely function. I was terrified. Getting through even one day was a tremendous effort. I made it to work but it was difficult. I didn't know where or who to turn to. To tell anyone what I was feeling was something I couldn't bring myself to do. As nearly as I can recall, this horrible dark cloud of despair lasted about a week, maybe longer, but at the time it seemed like an eternity. I didn't know where it came from or what was wrong with me. And then it passed as suddenly as it had come and I was ok again. A depression that severe didn't happen again for a couple of years.

While I was living in Nevada, I met my son's father who I eventually married and shortly thereafter I discovered I was pregnant.   Because of my prior surgery at age 17, I wasn't even sure that I could have a child so I was thrilled. Throughout my pregnancy I felt good; but right after my son was born, I was hit with my second major depression. Here I was with this beautiful baby boy who was both wanted and loved; yet again I was deeply depressed. At this time, I attributed it to the facts that we'd just moved from Nevada to Washington, I'd just quit a job I'd had for eight years, my husband traveled a great deal of the time, and I'd just had a baby. All those stress factors could cause anyone to get depressed, right?

As with my first major depression, this one lasted about 10 days; then there would be a reprieve of an indeterminate amount of time, and then it would come again out of the blue for no reason I could fathom. My husband didn't know what the hell was wrong with me; he wasn't understanding or supportive. I still couldn't understand why I felt this way and I was ashamed to tell anyone. Finally, at the recommendation of my obstetrician who felt it was postpartum depression—something many women experience after giving birth—I saw a psychiatrist who put me on an antidepressant. (Finally someone is actually trying to treat me with medication!) When I didn't respond immediately, lithium was added to the antidepressant and that seemed to provide some relief, but these mood episodes seemed to continue to have a life of their own regardless of what medications I was taking. I'd go through a few months feeling depressed off and on for several days at a time, and then a period of several months would pass, and I'd sail through, feeling fine.

Many doctors now believe that victims of depression carry an innate susceptibility to the disease. The disease itself can then be triggered by external factors or by a change in the body's own chemistry. Those who don't carry the gene are much less susceptible to ever experiencing depression.

When Darin was around 6 months old, I went back to work and things seemed to be ok for a while. I had one other serious depressive episode while I was working that lasted about ten days. I had just accepted a promotion to another job with the same company, but the day I was to start was the same day I was hit with the depression. I couldn't do it; I couldn't accept this promotion because at the time I was incapable of concentrating enough to learn something new. I was able to return to my original job, making some inane excuse as to why I couldn't make the change.

As with all depressive episodes, I didn't believe it would ever end, that I would ever make it through. I still didn't know a great deal about clinical depression, didn't know what caused it, didn't understand why I felt it, and didn't know how to make it go away.

I saw another psychiatrist who decided to try me on a monoamine oxidise inhibitor (MAOI). Although I did have to be careful with my diet and other medications, the Nardil I began taking did seem to alleviate my depressive symptoms, and I felt I'd found my panacea!

Several months passed and another job with the company became available. It was one I really wanted but it meant spending 6 weeks away from home in New York State for training, which would necessitate leaving my son at a very young age while I tried to advance my career. It was not an easy decision but when offered the job, I accepted. I felt a lot of guilt about leaving Darin for that amount of time. Six weeks to a toddler is a very long time to be away from his mother. And I missed him. I missed him a lot. Because of his father's job, which required a lot of traveling, Darin stayed a good deal of the time I was in New York at the home of the woman where he'd been going to daycare while I worked so not only was his mother gone, his dad was also absent much of the time.

I called him often while I was away. He wasn't talking yet, but I still felt it was important that he continued to hear my voice. I don't know if it made a difference but it was all I knew to do at the time. When I returned home after those 6 weeks, he was at first somewhat distant—as if he was angry with me for leaving him. Who could blame him? I was terribly afraid I might have caused him some permanent damage by my absence but after some time passed, we seemed to be back to normal.

As a pilot, Mark traveled a great deal, which was a huge stress on our marriage. In addition, he was extremely negative in his view of people, of things in general. When Darin was around three years old, Mark and I went through an ugly divorce and custody battle. Ugly. The morning we were due for our initial hearing, while I was feeding Darin baby cereal for breakfast, Mark took the bowl, poured it over Darin's head and said, "You clean it up," and walked out the door. When I went out to the garage to start my car so I could drop Darin off at daycare and then get to the hearing, my car wouldn't start. I managed to wake the neighbor next door and with his help, got it running. Later, Mark told me he'd turned on my car radio and left it on all night so the battery would be dead in the morning. He thought it was hilarious. I didn't.

Mark went to great lengths to gain sole custody of Darin. Going to all our neighbors' homes and asking them to write letters stating that they had seen him outside playing with Darin in the yard but had rarely, if ever, had they seen me outside with my son is an example. He tried in every way to sabotage me in our fight for custody. He retained a very clever attorney who somehow managed to convince my lawyer that although Washington is a community property state, I was not entitled to ½ of the assets. *Why is it that one person always seems to get the "killer" attorney in a divorce, while the other fares less well?* We eventually settled out of court because they had convinced me I would lose if we took it before a judge. He got the house, but more importantly, I retained custody of our son. I've since shredded all the paperwork; it was too depressing to keep.

Darin and I moved into an apartment and throughout the next three years, I experienced the normal ups and downs associated with a divorce and custody battle, but for reasons still unknown, I somehow escaped the horror of a severe depression. Go figure. I could go into a depression for no fathomable reason and yet when it seemed I really did have a reason, I escaped unscathed. I did have many difficult moments, but not the kind that rendered me completely helpless. I could still function.

Mark didn't know anything about depression, didn't understand it. He hadn't understood it throughout our marriage. For that, I can't blame him; many people don't. At one point following our divorce, he did tell me that he'd read a pamphlet about depression and that he was sorry he hadn't understood. I respected him for caring enough to finally make an attempt to understand.

There did, however, continue to be a great deal of animosity between my son's father and me. Although Darin was both wanted and loved by both his parents, the animosity we exhibited toward each other did not go unnoticed by our son, and I know he suffered for it. I do not claim to have been totally innocent of making negative comments here and there about his father; and Darin was well aware of how his father felt about me. He once asked, "Mommy, why is my Dad so mean at you?"

I wanted to make the best home for him that I possibly could. I loved him more than anything else and I wanted him to have the kind of childhood I never had. I knew he couldn't get the love and support at daycare that I could have given him at home, but it was necessary that I work; therefore I had no choice.

A memory of that period still haunts me: As I had done many times, I was dropping Darin off in the morning on my way to work. This particular morning he started to cry the minute I got in my car to leave. Picture this precious little 4-year-old hanging onto the inside of a chain-link fence as I was driving away, screaming, "Mommy, mommy," with tears streaming down his face. After I drove away, I pulled over and sat for a few minutes trying to decide what to do. God, how I wanted to go back, pick him up and take him home. But I couldn't because of appointments I was obligated to keep. It broke my heart. I remember that incident to this day and it was more than 25 years ago. Guilt doesn't get any better than that.

In spite of all the obstacles, Darin and I did pretty well. I believe I was a good mother and that he always knew he was loved. Years later he shared with me that some of his best memories were of our time in that apartment.

Some three years after the divorce, through my job, I met Jacob. He was everything I thought I ever wanted. He adored me, and my son. At least I thought so at the time. And I believe I truly loved him. He asked me to marry him on our second or third date. Don't you think that after two failed marriages I might have learned not to jump right in? Well, you'd be wrong.

Obviously, knowing each other for such a relatively short time, there were things neither of us recognized—things about ourselves we probably should have known—but we rushed right in anyway.

Things were fine for a while until we both began to figure out the other wasn't quite as perfect as we'd originally thought. We were like night and day. Whereas I was emotional, he was stoic; I loved to dance, he didn't; he operated on logic, I used feelings. There were simply too many differences. Not entirely his fault and not entirely mine. I do realize I still carried some of that old "...wouldn't want to belong to any club that would have me as a member" mentality, which didn't help in forming any real closeness. When I truly thought I was loved and needed, there remained somewhere deep down inside, that little girl who still believed she didn't deserve it.

After a year of marriage, we moved to California for reasons to do with Jacob's business. I quit my job of eight years. I desperately wanted this marriage to work. I don't know what he wanted. To this day I don't know; I probably never will.

While we lived in California, I was like mother of the year, or at least tried to be. I was a soccer mom, helped him with Cub Scouts and attended all his softball games, the whole 9 yards. Things were good. Except for my marriage. And the depressions.

Following our move and subsequent to my first major depression while living in California, I saw a psychiatrist who increased the dosage of the MAOI that I was taking and added lithium. There were periods during the next 6 years when I believed myself to be "cured," that at last they had found the right medication; that my brain chemistry had miraculously returned to normal. I went back to college and concurrent with a psychology course I took, even wrote a couple of papers on depression and the medications commonly used to treat it.

Throughout the next 6 years I experienced two or three major depressions that each lasted a couple of weeks. Jacob was not understanding or supportive through my depressive episodes. He despised weakness and that's what he thought this was: weakness. For the most part, he ignored it—and me—while I crawled through these episodes. He found his escape in his work. He also traveled a great bit and was usually gone most of the week but home on weekends. I did at times *contemplate* suicide though I never had a real plan. I do remember telling him that if something should happen to me, please take care of Darin. But the awful depressions eventually passed, and I survived.

I can't express strongly enough how debilitating depression can be. One time Darin had a friend coming from Seattle to stay with us for a few days and I had planned to take them to Alcatraz and to one of piers in San Francisco. A few days before he arrived, I was struck with yet another visit from hell. Couldn't go through with it, couldn't bear to even leave the house. I asked Jacob if he would take them, and God bless him, he did. Another horrible part of ongoing depression that comes and goes is being unable to plan anything ahead because you never know what condition you'll be in at any time. It's happened more than once. I'd plan something, like having a friend come to visit, and maybe a week or so before she'd come, another episode would manifest itself.

After almost seven years, Jacob's and my marriage began to really deteriorate. Things went from bad to worse. We hardly talked to each other. He had always been aloof, but now he was more distant than ever. I couldn't reach him. And I tried. I was aware that I was partly to blame for the failure of this relationship but he simply refused to discuss it. He had somehow managed to forever shut me out and there was no way I could get back in. Do people do that to protect themselves or to punish the other person? I don't know.

He began spending more time away than at home and I finally asked if there was someone else. He said absolutely not. I believed him. I truly believed he was not the kind of person who would cheat.

In addition to the psychiatrist I was seeing for medication, I was also in therapy with a psychologist, partly in an effort to figure out why my marriages never seemed to work and partly to try and find an answer and a solution to the depressions that always seemed just over the horizon.

Then I discovered Jacob really *was* having an affair with a woman who worked for him in his new office in Arizona. I was devastated. I wanted to work it out. He wanted a legal separation. Why a legal separation and not a divorce? We were in California. It's a community property state. With a legal separation he could put all his business assets in his name only while still married to me, thus I would have no access to them when we divorced. Cunning? It was several years before I figured that one out. Naïve would be an understatement. I simply cannot believe that I was so blind to so much for so long. I even agreed to share an attorney!

We put the house on the market, obtained a legal separation, and he moved permanently to Arizona. When the house sold in June of 1991, I arranged to have our belongings packed and Darin and I moved back to the Seattle area, bought a home, and waited for the moving truck to arrive. It was a difficult time for him at best. I'd moved him from Seattle to California and now back to Seattle. He loved where we lived in California. He was so happy there. He was popular and well liked. But I hoped that the fact that his father lived in Seattle would at least make the adjustment easier on him. Only one of the many errors in judgment I was to make over the new few years.

Shortly after arriving back in Seattle, but prior to moving in our house, I drove Darin to his dad's to see him. I sat in Mark's kitchen and told him what had happened with Jacob and me. His reply was, "If this had happened sooner, we could have gotten back together." He was soooooo understanding and comforting. Ah, but he was already remarried. And that was the end of that—even if I'd considered it—which I didn't.

About the time Darin and I were moving into our house, the depression came with a vengeance. I couldn't bear to think about unpacking, moving in, anything. The moving truck arrived with our furniture and household goods but all I could do for days was look at the unpacked boxes and shuffle Darin around in an effort to spare him the trauma of seeing his mother completely immobile. In addition to failing at one more marriage, I was overwhelmed with yet another occurrence of this devastating illness. Who could I call? Who could help me? Where could I turn? I could, at least, attribute the onset of this particular episode to going through a divorce, getting "dumped," but that didn't make it any easier.

I spent many days right after our move back just getting out of bed, managing to take a shower and dress, sometimes driving around in my car, parking in a lot in a strip mall and simply sitting there for most of the day. I was afraid of being completely by myself. Sometimes I'd go over to my old neighbor's home, usually in the evening, and just sit there watching TV with her and her daughter. As long as someone was physically with me, I wasn't as panicky. They didn't even have to talk to me; just allow me to be with someone so I wasn't completely alone. I didn't want the neighbors who lived in my neighborhood to see me because I couldn't carry on a halfway intelligent conversation; and I was afraid they would think I was crazy, or worse. Is there anything worse? I don't think so. And at that point in time, I *was* crazy. I couldn't eat. I was losing weight rapidly. I was in a living nightmare. I didn't think I had *ever* been this terrified.

I hadn't found a therapist in Washington so I was still dependent on the psychologist I had been seeing in California. He had told me that I could call him until I found someone to work with in my new location. I was frightened and desperate. After leaving him several frantic messages with no returned calls, I finally reached him and asked, "Why haven't you returned my calls?"

He snapped back, "Because I'm busy. I'm working. Why haven't you found another therapist?" I said, "I've seen one person but I'm not sure she can help me." He retorted, "Well she's responsible for you now." He said he was no longer an option and I could no longer call him. I was totally freaked out. Add panic to depression and it's like having your skin peeled off. Remember also that we're talking about a woman who, at the time, had no self-esteem. Whatever little I did have was wiped out by the depression.

This episode of depression completely destroyed my ability to think rationally. It distorted my thinking and my perceptions so completely that everything seemed much worse than it actually was. Or maybe it was that bad. Every wrong that I felt had been committed against me was magnified in my mind so utterly that I couldn't cope. Any self-esteem I had gained over the years was completely absent. I was so needy, so desperate for some crumb of evidence from Jacob that he at least cared what was happening to me that I was completely out of control. I felt as if my world had been pulled out from under me. I vacillated between hating him and needing him. I made frequent, desperate phone calls to him. I cried. I groveled. I practically begged him to love me. I did absolutely insane things. I called his girlfriend and hung up on her. I called him and hung up. I called him three, four times a day and each time I called, the nastier and colder he became. I couldn't seem to stop reaching out in desperation for someone who wanted nothing to do with me. *Was I crazy or what?* I couldn't get a grip. My marriage, which I had hoped would be for the rest of my life, was unredeemable. The stability I had hoped to have finally found for both myself and Darin was no longer an option. I was lost. I was afraid. I had no anchor.

I'd always thought of myself as a reasonably strong person considering what I'd already survived. Don't misunderstand. I'm not having a pity party here. *Well, at the time, maybe I was.* But I do know there are others who've been through and survived much more than I.

It was paramount that Darin not feel a responsibility for now taking care of *me.* I was the mother; he was the child. He needed me to be strong and I was unable to be. I was in the midst of a devastating depression, completely out of control, and even I couldn't understand what was happening.

It was like a black cloud that suddenly, without warning, enveloped me, separating me from the rest of the world. Nothing mattered to me. Things I once enjoyed had no meaning. Life had no meaning. All hope was gone. I couldn't eat, I could barely move. Self-esteem became non-existent. I couldn't remember the person I used to be, couldn't believe I'd ever feel normal again. The only thing I cared about was my son. I tried as much as I was able to hide it from him, but I didn't do a spectacular job. Twelve year olds aren't stupid. They know when something is wrong.

I couldn't cook, I couldn't work, I couldn't enjoy a movie, I couldn't clean house, I couldn't do laundry, I couldn't pay bills. The longer it continued, the more panicked I became. My body was alive but my mind was frozen somewhere dark and terrifying from where I couldn't escape.

Several years later I was in a psychologist's office telling him about that period of my life—what had happened to me in Seattle when I lost custody of my son, the time spent in psychiatric wards, how I had wanted to kill myself—and he said to me, "You had a complete nervous breakdown." "Wow," I said. "I always wondered what a nervous breakdown was. And that's what it was?"

I spent a great deal of time at Marsha and Roger's, a couple I'd known for many years. They allowed me to stay at their home, listened to my ramblings, and fed me what little I was able to eat. They kept me alive. They certainly didn't know what to do to take me through this but they were at least kind enough to give me a place to stay and offer what support they were able. And I do know that having someone living with you—even part-time—who is suffering from severe depression, is no piece of cake. It disrupts their lives and affects them greatly.

I know there were times I leaned too heavily on a few people. I completely overwhelmed them with my neediness. For a while, I leaned too heavily on my son's father and his new wife. At first they were supportive and seemed to be compassionate, but after too many terrified early morning phone calls and too many times of calling and asking Darin's father to please come and pick him up because I couldn't cope, they backed away and left me to cope on my own. I completely overwhelmed them with my neediness. That much I can understand and accept. But what they did later is unconscionable.

One day while I was at their house I noticed a yellow legal pad with my name on it. I picked it up, and before his wife, Jean, had time to grab it from my hand, I saw enough to realize they were taking notes on me, and my behavior. Something was definitely up. And something said to me: "Be afraid. Be very afraid."

I lost some friends because of my illness. There were those who couldn't deal with someone who was depressing to be around, who contributed nothing, who only clung desperately, calling at all hours of the day and night in absolute terror crying out for help. They couldn't understand and they didn't know how to help.

Although strides have been made, the stigma that has been associated with depression and manic depression still separates us from the rest of the community. Many people still seem to believe you can just "pull yourself together." They don't seem to understand that it is a *chemical imbalance* of neurotransmitters in the brain. It is a *physical disorder*. Physical disorders appear to be genetically transmitted, cannot be caught like mumps, and—like diabetes— require constant watchfulness and appropriate treatment.

One friend I'd known for a very long time suddenly stopped returning my calls or responding to my notes. The only conclusion I can come to is that the last time I saw her was soon after my first series of ECT—a time I was at the high end of hypomania and my behavior was perhaps a little bizarre. Fact is, I'm sure it was more than a little bizarre. But still, she knew something about what I was going through. I don't think I'll ever fully understand. When you lose a friend because of something you really have no control over, it's a hurt than doesn't easily go away. At times I tend to blame myself because I behaved in a way that alienated someone I believed was a friend and I mourn that loss. Rejection hurts, no matter what the reason. But I know it was something I couldn't change regardless of how much I wish I could.

There were, however, a rare few who stood by me when it wasn't easy to do so. One of those very special persons was my best friend, Laura. I've known Laura for years—since all three of our kids were toddlers, long before we'd moved from Seattle to California. We're still best friends. Without her unquestioning friendship during many, many dark times, I'm not certain I could have endured. She's been through a great deal of pain in her own life; and compared to her childhood, mine was a walk in the park. We've always been there for each other, through good and bad.

Because depression is categorized as a mental illness, and mental illness seems to frighten many people because of the reputation it carries, it's difficult for many to treat those of us with depression as an equal. Avoidance and denial are abundant and somewhat accepted in society; mental illness is another ballgame. Mental illness—which includes depression and manic depression—carries with it a stigma that many times causes others to treat the person experiencing it as if they were somehow guilty of being on less than an equal intellectual or social status with the rest of society.

Is a person suffering from depressive illness not entitled to the same courtesy and respect as someone not similarly stricken? Because a person has been unfortunate enough to have been afflicted and diagnosed with depression instead of diabetes or heart disease, should they be relegated to a category that somehow places them on a less than equal stratum?

No one chooses depression any more than one chooses to have cancer. Of those of us who have been diagnosed with depression or bipolar disorder, many of us have suffered much from the ignorance of those who fear to look at what we have seen, who don't wish to acknowledge or discuss it, try to change the subject, or simply avoid any further contact with us. It hurts.

Although we have been broken, we have somehow managed to pick up the pieces and try to put them back together. There is something important to be learned here, both for those who have suffered and those who seek to help us. We must teach each other.

While I was staying at Marsha and Roger's, who were already aware of what was going on with me (*that I'd completely lost my mind*), Laura brought her two kids over and unpacked and set up my living room so there was at least one room in the house that wasn't full of boxes. Another time she brought her son over and he mowed the grass for me. That, in my estimation, is real friendship. You don't find that often. When you do, cherish it.

Finally, after 25 days of living among mostly unpacked boxes, I had a brief respite of two or three days. I suddenly felt normal again! The paralyzing darkness simply lifted as if someone had snapped their fingers and it was gone. I swear that's how it often happened with me.

I started to unpack boxes, hang pictures, set up my computer and make beds. I stayed up all night because I knew I had to get as much done as possible in case the depression returned. And a few days later it did.

Darin was 12 years old. He couldn't possibly understand what was happening; he'd never seen me like this. I was a walking zombie who could do no more than shower and dress every day. Anything beyond that was impossible. I managed to have him stay with Laura and her two kids or at his Dad's much of the time because I didn't want him to continually observe how utterly frightened and out-of-control I was. It wasn't that I didn't want him or that I didn't want to take care of him; it was because in the state I was in, I couldn't even take care of myself.

The first of July 1991, I had a gynecologist appointment. I parked in front, got out of my car and started toward the building. I don't know if it was the heat of the day combined with the medication I was on or what, but I got very dizzy and fell down in front of the door to the doctor's office. Someone helped me inside and the nurse came out and talked to me. I fell apart. I was crying. I told her I was depressed, that I wanted to die, that I was desperate and confused. She took me into the doctor's office and they suggested that I let her drive me to Overlake Hospital in Bellevue to check into the psychiatric unit. I agreed, hoping that someone who dealt with this illness on a daily basis could finally help me.

I was admitted to the psychiatric unit on July 2, 1991 and released on July 5. This was to be my first of three hospitalizations for depression in the course of two years. Sitting there crying, waiting to be checked in, one of the nurses on staff came over and sat down. She said, "You have to be strong. Clinical depression sometimes lasts for 18 months before a remission." That was reassuring. It might be 18 months before I felt any relief? If this was the case, I knew I wouldn't be alive in 18 months. That wouldn't be something I'd say to a severely depressed person even if it were true. That would be enough to cause some people to run out in front of a semi.

The psychiatrist I was assigned to at Overlake increased the dosage of the antidepressant I was taking to the maximum recommended. I was on Nardil, an MAO inhibitor that falls in one category of antidepressants with which you have to be very careful. Combining an MAO inhibitor with many other medications—particularly Demerol—can sometimes have severe consequences. There are also dietary restrictions. Because of the side effects, it's usually not the first antidepressant of choice. It does, however, work for many people when other anti-depressants have failed.

Dr. Robinson treated me like a *person*. He was caring and supportive—there have been many who were not. He offered me *hope and encouragement* and I was treated with respect. At the time I didn't fully appreciate what an essential part of hospitalization a caring doctor can mean until later when I was in another facility and was assigned the doctor from hell. When a person is so severely depressed they are exempt of any hope, it's imperative to feel that your doctor wants to help! Crucial.

I didn't like being in a psychiatric ward. *Like some people do?* However, Overlake was one of the better ones. I can't think of anyone there who didn't treat the patients with respect. I went to group therapy, I ate what I could manage, but my depression didn't go away. I wish I could be more descriptive but I wasn't journaling then and it was so long ago that I've forgotten much. The hospital is not a cure. It's a safe place to be when you're feeling out of control, when you can't do anything for yourself, when you're feeling suicidal.

A portion of the Discharge Diagnosis written by the psychiatrist at Overlake—and this is important because it differs so dramatically from the one written by the doctor from hell who I would be assigned to upon my next hospitalization yet to come, reads:

The patient presented as a casually dressed, well-groomed, thin, white female who presented with a superficially bright affect and was obviously self-conscious and anxious... she was embarrassed about being hospitalized... she presented her history in a coherent fashion, and manifested tight associations... she is very aware of her inappropriate dependency needs...I believe a short hospitalization would be most beneficial for this patient...keeping her hospitalizations short would probably be most helpful to the patient.

When my doctor no longer felt I was a suicide risk, I was released and I went to Laura's where Darin was already staying. I was still very depressed. Laura and I and the kids went to a big water park one day. She thought it would be good for me to get out and the kids loved the place. Laura packed some lunch, and we headed out. I remember that all I could do was lie on the blanket in some kind of stupor. I couldn't even eat anything—no appetite whatsoever. The kids had a great time going down the slides and when they came back to where we were sitting to eat lunch, it was obvious I was off in some dark world of my own. Darin asked Laura, "What's wrong with my mom?" She told him I was just feeling down. God, that was an awful time for him. He knew I wasn't myself and he didn't know why.

As I write this and think back to those times, it's difficult for me to even imagine feeling that kind of total despair. I remember it, but if it hadn't happened to me, I wouldn't believe anyone could feel such complete emptiness and isolation. Martha Manning said it perfectly in her book, *Undercurrents*: "Depression is like being in hell with only your name on the door."

While staying with Laura, I ruminated constantly about killing myself. I was at the point where I believed the only way out of this gut-wrenching emotional pain was to kill myself because I wasn't going to ever get better. I was obsessed with finding a way out.

I went through the knife drawer in her kitchen. There was nothing sharp enough that I could use to slit my wrists. I saw some prescription bottles on her kitchen counter and found a bottle of Tranxene®. It was full so I put 15 or 20 in my pocket. That night around midnight, I quickly scribbled a suicide note to Laura and to Darin apologizing for what I was going to do. I didn't even have the strength to write a decent suicide note; it was just a couple of lines scribbled in pencil. I went out to the garage, took the pills out of my pocket and just looked at them, trying to convince myself to get in my car and drive somewhere and take them. I would never kill myself in someone's home; what an awful, thoughtless act that would be. *Killing myself and leaving my son without a mother wouldn't be an awful, thoughtless act?*

There was still the fear that I might end up a vegetable in an institution the rest of my life. As much as I wanted, I just couldn't talk myself into doing it.

Laura heard me downstairs, came out to the garage and asked me what I was doing. She took the pills out of my hand, and was furious with me. She asked me how many I'd taken. I told her, "only two." It was the truth. She made me come inside and told me I had to go back to the hospital. I told her no, they couldn't help me. She foraged the yellow pages, looking for some other place I might go for help. She found a private psychiatric hospital in Kirkland, reasoned that since it was a private psychiatric hospital, it might be better equipped to help me. Major mistake.

The next morning Laura made me get out of bed and dress—not an easy task when I was still knocked out from the Tranxene®—then drove me to Fairfax Hospital with all three kids in the car. She couldn't just leave them home alone. Can you imagine how frightened Darin must have been? He was only 12! And I was so messed up I barely knew what was happening.

The woman at the front desk—not a very nice person—asked me if I wanted to stay. I told her I didn't know. There was no hint of any compassion, as I would have expected of someone in her position. I was looking for hope, help, and encouragement. I wanted someone to tell me they could help me! This woman then yelled at someone in the back to "call the State Mental Health" and send someone over to question me. That's when I realized they were going to try to have me committed involuntarily. I was panicked! I told her I'd stay. She said, "no, it's too late, the State's already been called." That's when I got really scared. Really, really scared.

They took me back in the bowels of the place and stuck me in "lockup" where Laura sat with me until the man from the State Mental Health Department came. He was at least kind, more than I can say for anyone else I'd talked to so far. I was honest. I told the man I was very depressed and wished I were dead. I didn't say I wanted to kill myself—just that I wished I were dead. *Is there a difference?*

Before asking me any questions, he warned me to be careful about what I said because whatever I said he'd have to report. I just wanted someone to help me so badly that I just blurted out what I felt. I was halfway clueless about what was happening, but I was smart enough to know it wasn't good.

After he left, the hospital administrator—who it turns out was the *real nice woman* I'd encountered at the front desk—informed me that unless I could come up with $6,000 for my first 72 hours, they would send me to the State Hospital, which I envisioned was a lot like the one in *One Flew over the Cuckoo's Nest.* They were holding me against my will and if I didn't come up with $6,000 immediately, they'd just ship me off and let the State handle it. While I was desperately trying to find a way to get the money, I was left in "lockup" for the first 24 hours—a horrifying experience to say the least. There were two other people in lockup—a woman who walked around half naked mumbling to herself, and a man I don't remember much about.

The first thing I was told the next morning was that I was going to court to testify on my own behalf and if the judge felt I was a danger to myself, I could be locked up indefinitely. *And telling me this was going to help me act "normal" in front of a judge?*

Give me a reason to want to live? Wouldn't you just kinda get the feeling they wanted the money and if you didn't have it, tough shit? They'd just ship you off to a State institution where God knows what would happen?

As God is my witness, I swear that everything I'm saying here is the absolute truth and not embellished in the slightest.

Before someone took me to court, I was allowed to take a shower in a stall with no door in a room that was cold and water that was cold. I asked for a hairdryer but was refused because of the danger I might use it in a suicide attempt. *If I could've killed myself, I'd have done it by now with better things than a hairdryer.*

I tried to dress as well as I could so the judge would see that I wasn't crazy and lock me up. No way in hell did I want to stay in this awful place where I was treated not much better than a stray animal, but the way I saw it, I only had two options: Convince them to let me stay voluntarily, or take the risk of going to court and being declared a danger to myself; (I *had* written two suicide notes which Laura had given them when she first brought me in) then be sent to the State hospital which I knew nothing about except for the horror stories I'd heard. *In hindsight, it might not have been much worse than this torture* *chamber and it wouldn't cost me $6,000 but I couldn't take that chance.*

I reduced myself to *begging*, until the hospital finally relented, about 30 minutes before I was scheduled to leave for the courthouse, and allowed me to sign the papers admitting myself voluntarily. I did, of course, have to pay the $6,000 up front before they'd even consider allowing me to stay. At least if I was a voluntary patient, I might be able to figure out what to do without the fear of being institutionalized forever.

The room alone, which I shared with three other people, was $600 a night. I was forced to go to several "group therapy" sessions a day, which were all an additional charge.

Although they were aware I'd been in the psychiatric ward at Overlake Hospital less than a week prior to admission to this fun place, I was given every blood test and medical test they could think of to charge me for. No attempt was made to obtain copies of results of the identical tests I was now being given a 2nd time. *If they had, they couldn't charge me a 2nd time; that makes sense.*

They charged me for three EKG's because *their* equipment didn't work correctly for the first two! *Oh yes, I've kept the discharge papers and bills from both places.* It was a very bad joke! I was a prisoner in a $600 a night psychiatric hospital where no one, other than a couple of the other patients and one aide, seemed to have any compassion for anyone. I had no medical insurance, thus I had to pay cash. Thank God I had it. They flashed a flashlight in my face a couple times a night to make sure I hadn't killed myself. After all, they were legally responsible. I had no energy or motivation to fight back. I had no idea what they might be able to do to me if I were anything but completely compliant. I was afraid that if I wasn't compliant, they might put me back in lockup again.

No one on staff, with the exception of the aide, exhibited the smallest amount of compassion or took any time to talk with me. I was utterly terrified and, needless to say, I didn't get better. Once again, I was in hell. Only this time, it was real.

I believe there are competent, caring people out there who do want to help, but for me, finding them then was a hit-or-miss situation. There were even some who, in the beginning, led me to believe they could help, but as time went on and I didn't get better, they seemed to give up and yet didn't have the integrity to admit they were stumped and suggest an alternative.

Try to imagine how you would feel if you suddenly found yourself completely out of control of your thoughts and feelings. Then imagine how desperate you might become if you reached the point that you truly felt *no one* was going to be able to help you. If *they* were professionals, and *they* were giving up on you, how could you possibly keep yourself going?

Finally, two days after being admitted, they told me I was going to see a psychiatrist on their staff. I was assigned the doctor from hell. (I'll call him Dr. Sand.) This was two days *after* my admission; two days that I spent in "lockup" without benefit of speaking with a doctor or even a social worker. Two days for which I was being charged and nobody was doing anything but keeping me locked up. When I was finally allowed to see Dr. Sand, it was intuitively obvious from the moment I entered his office and sat down that he couldn't have cared less about me, or much of anything I had to say. He made no attempt to even treat me in a kind manner. He was on the edge of hostile; I recognize contempt when I see it.

Following my release from this place, and upon reading his evaluation reports, I discovered the major part of the reason: Before Dr. Sand had even spoken to me, my ex-husband—Darin's father—had called the hospital and spoken to him. It appears that Dr. Sand's evaluation of me was based entirely on the flagrant and deliberate misrepresentations made by my former husband.

The following is quoted, verbatim, from my evaluation and discharge papers written by Dr. Sand:

After being in the hospital, the patient refused to remain...In the course of the day, one of the patient's four ex-husbands contacted the hospital and indicated that the patient has a history of being manipulative, has had in the past multiple doctors and is capable of considerable manipulation, and other suicide notes were found...The patient appears to be minimizing to some extent, and has a history of manipulative behaviors.

Allow me to respond to these statements:

- I did *not* refuse to remain. I even stated to the extremely hateful woman at the front desk (in the presence of my friend, Laura) that I would agree to stay, at which point I was informed by this woman that it was too late. I was now at their mercy. I sure as hell didn't want to be there, but when given the option of signing papers to voluntarily admit myself or be sent to the State Hospital, I obviously chose to stay.
- I did *not* have four ex-husbands as stated by my son's father. I had two ex-husbands and was separated from my 3rd.
- I have never been accused of manipulative behavior by "numerous doctors" or by *any*

doctors for that matter; and I do not have a "history of manipulative behavior." Not then, not ever.

- Numerous suicide notes were found? Where? When? By whom? Completely false.

Dr. Sand did not speak with any of my "previous" doctors, not even the doctor who had treated me at Overlake Hospital. He did not even ask for any names of previous doctors although I did tell him the doctor's name at Overlake Hospital. It is so stated in his report. And I do still have in my possession his report.

Darin's father came to visit me at Fairfax, expressing great concern and caring. Under the guise of having only my well being in mind, he persistently urged me to sign a release allowing him to speak with my doctor so he could supposedly help me get out of there. At the time, I believed him. I wanted to. In actuality, he and his new wife, Jean, were preparing a case against me in an attempt to prove my incompetence for reasons I will never in this lifetime understand.

Dr. Sand based his "history of manipulative behavior" and "other suicide notes were found" on what someone said who had absolutely no credentials to assess my medical condition, or even speak about it. My ex-husband was never planning to help me. Is it any wonder I still harbor some bitterness?

It is incomprehensible to me that another human being with any conscience could pretend to want to help, to be a shoulder to lean on, while covertly attacking the mother of his child in such a cruel and vicious manner.

Again I want to avow that all of the above along with the quotations from my doctor's evaluations are the absolute truth, verifiable by journal entries I maintained and by copies of the actual discharge papers from these hospitals. What right did this man have to base his diagnosis on whatever crap my ex-husband told him? Dr. Sand also stated in his evaluation that I would be given one-on-one therapy. That never happened.

Some have asked why I didn't sue. In actuality, at the time, I was in no condition to fight back. I didn't have the strength; I was in the middle of a nervous breakdown. During my stay, I talked to other women who were either like myself—extremely depressed and felt they weren't getting the help they needed—or else they were younger women who were staying there on insurance money because they had no other place to go.

A woman patient I spoke to who was from Canada, told me she had attempted suicide seven times! I mean really tried—not just half-ass tried like

I had. She had the scars on her wrists to prove it. I can't state this strongly enough: If you have been admitted to a psychiatric hospital—involuntarily—they can do almost anything to you and you have absolutely no control over it. Why? Because you are "crazy" and no one will believe anything you say. I'm not saying it's something that happens all the time, but it *does* happen. More than it should. Not as much as it has in the past, but it *does* happen. At least it happened to me 16 years ago, and it was the most awful experience imaginable.

I realized that if I were ever going to get out of this place—because it was intuitively obvious they weren't even trying to help me—I had to at least make think I was getting better. I began telling Dr. Sand that I was feeling better, that I needed to get home and start my life again; that I needed to get my son enrolled in school. And yes, I confess, this time I was lying—I wasn't getting better—I just wanted out of this awful place.

I remember the day I was released like it was yesterday. There was one young girl who had been admitted the day before. I'd sort of taken her under my wing because she was scared. I showed her where the cafeteria was, helped her get food, talked with her some, and gave her what little encouragement I was able to offer. I simply tried to be her friend because I could see the same fear in her eyes that I had in my own. When I told her I was checking out, she was so afraid. "What will I do without you?" she asked me. I felt so badly about leaving her. She was so alone. And I knew what that felt like. Even in my own pain I was able to care about someone else who might feel worse than I.

When it was time for me to leave, my friend's husband, Roger, came to pick me up. I remember starting with my bag toward the unlocked area of the place and I thought I was going to pass out or fall down; afraid I wouldn't make it to the door and thus they wouldn't let me go. I prayed silently, "Please, God, just let me get out the door."

When I got to their house, I actually managed to eat dinner, which they commented on. But the main reason I was able to eat was that I wanted them to think I was ok and capable of going home. My plan, once again, was to find a way to kill myself. Darin was staying with his dad and stepmother so I figured this was as good a time as any. I had to figure out how the hell to do it. I thought about taking the bottle of antidepressant medication I had but I wasn't sure the pills would kill me—they might simply cause me to hallucinate or have a seizure. *I do believe there are worse things than being dead.*

Hanging myself was out; I wouldn't know the first thing about tying a knot and I didn't even have a rope. Besides the garage was too full of boxes to find any room to set it up. Slash my wrists? That might work. After scouring the house for razor blades, I finally located one single-edge razor blade. I made myself a drink—for fortification—and sat down on the sofa. I made a cut on my left wrist. It hurt! I tried it again. It seriously hurt like hell. How do people actually do this? Are they oblivious to pain? *At the time I didn't realize that you were supposed to slash your wrists in the bathtub.* I couldn't push the blade in hard enough to sever a vein because it hurt too damn much. I couldn't even remember which way the cut was supposed to go to succeed. Was it vertically or horizontally? I so badly wanted to die and yet so cowardly I couldn't endure the pain it would take to do it.

I was determined to kill myself if it took all night. Next I decided I'd get in my car, drive across the Mercer Island Bridge, park my car, and jump off into Lake Washington. By this time it was 2:30 in the morning and there wouldn't be any traffic. That was a bonus. Great plan. I got in my car, drove to the bridge, then drove back and forth across it three or four times trying to get up the courage to pull over and jump. I pulled over once, got out of my car and looked over into the water. I considered all the reasons this wouldn't work: What if the water was too shallow at that spot? What if I didn't drown? What if someone saw me and pulled me out? Time was running short. It was going to be daylight before too much longer. Traffic would be starting across the bridge. I had to do it soon or forget it.

I remembered a beach I used to go to in Bellevue. Maybe I could drown myself there. So I headed to Bellevue and looked for the beach. There were a couple of new houses that hadn't been there when I was there several years before which made it impossible to just walk into the water; I had to get to it first. I parked my car down the road, climbed over a fence into someone's back yard, which gave me access to what I thought would be the deepest part of the lake, eased myself into the water and tried to swim out as far I could. Not only was it just a little hard to swim because I was wearing jeans and a sweatshirt, but the water was also too shallow and it was freezing cold.

Understand that although I thought I wanted to die, I wanted it to be easy; nothing was going right to make this easy. OK, even if I did manage to drown, which was highly unlikely because I couldn't seem to get far enough out in the water, I got to thinking that drowning would not be a real pleasant way to go; sucking water into your lungs. Finally, I gave up in desperation, climbed back over the fence praying no one would see me sneaking through their back yard and shoot me (*which would have solved my current dilemma, except with my luck, I'd only be wounded and hauled off to jail*), and walked back to my car. Dripping wet, I drove home, went in the house and wrapped myself in a blanket and sat on the sofa. I didn't have the energy to change into dry clothes. First, I'd have to find some; then I'd have to remove the wet ones; then I'd have to change into the dry ones. It was too much effort. So I sat on the sofa and tried to figure out what to do next.

The next morning I got out the yellow pages and called gun shops. I discovered there was a 5-day waiting period to purchase a gun in the state. I'd have to wait 5 days?

I called an old friend in Colorado in a panic and told her I wanted to kill myself. She was concerned and talked to me for quite a while; but several months later she changed her phone number because she was going through some pretty heavy stuff herself and couldn't deal with mine, too. Depression *does* sometimes drive people away. Sad, but true.

And then, of course, because I hadn't quite humiliated myself enough, I called Jacob for about the hundredth time and told him I was really, really suicidal. *That sounds a bit masochistic doesn't it?* Needless to say, that was a dead end.

Because I couldn't purchase a gun in the state without a Washington I.D. and I didn't have time to get a new driver's license, I went some place where I was able to get a picture I.D. The following day I drove to a gun shop, applied for a gun permit, and waited the five days to purchase it. I thought I'd finally hit pay dirt. Anyone could shoot herself, right? How hard could it be? There'd be only a second's worth of pain.

Fortunately, by the time I picked up the gun, I began to feel a little better, so I decided to wait and see if the depression was lifting. It did, for a while— almost two weeks! When not depressed, I was actually a rational, functioning, productive person. I think it's pretty clear by now that I never really wanted to die. No one really does. I just wanted to be well; but I didn't believe that would ever happen. Had I been truly serious about killing myself, I would have done it. A bullet through the head is a pretty sure way: quick, and relatively painless. Or so I would assume.

At the recommendation of a friend, I began seeing a counselor in Bellevue. Unfortunately for me, this was a mistake that would have enormous negative consequences on the rest of my life, and my son's. Greg wasn't even a certified therapist or mental health care professional. He had absolutely no credentials to be treating someone suffering with severe, recurring depression. Only after the damage had been done did I discover this.

During a period when I was in a somewhat better state of mind, but still without my head on straight, I began to believe that I had made a terrible mistake moving back to Seattle. Maybe we should have stayed in California. Darin was happy there. He never wanted to leave. I was the one who decided we should return to Seattle. I put the house in Bellevue up for sale. I told myself that if it was meant to be that we should go back to California, the house would sell, and if not, it wouldn't. *Where did I come up with that?*

I flew to California to look for a place to live. The moment I arrived, I knew it was a mistake. First of all, everything in California was more expensive. Secondly, how could I possibly make rational decisions when I was on an emotional roller coaster? I told Darin we couldn't move back, that we couldn't afford it. God, I can't believe all that kid went through. But the worst hadn't even begun.

By the time I realized there wasn't anything affordable in California, the house in Bellevue sold and I found another house in Kirkland, bought it, and moved in. Now my reasoning became that the mortgage was really more than I could have afforded when the alimony ended anyway, so I would be better off with a smaller, less expensive house. My moods were completely erratic; one minute I felt great and the next I wanted to die. I'd just had a nervous breakdown, spent time in two psychiatric wards, and I'm buying and selling houses. I found another, less expensive house in Kirkland; and was able to get moved in with the help, again, of the same friends.

In the meantime, while still seeing Greg for "therapy," I began to see a psychiatrist in Seattle, Dr. Harris. When I told Dr. Harris about Greg and his so-called therapy, he admonished me that anyone could hang out a shingle and call himself a therapist. He referred to Greg as a "toy doctor" and did not believe Greg could help me. He was right on that one. If only I'd listened. I believe that if I'd stayed with Dr. Harris, followed his advice, some of the hell I went through later would have been avoided.

I think I stopped seeing Dr. Harris because he told me truths that I didn't want to hear. I had been seeing a married man. Although at the time this "relationship" began, he told me he was divorced. Now a normal person would have shown him the door, but I was not a "normal" person right then; so I continued to see him even after I discovered the truth. Yes, it was very self-destructive, but I was so incredibly lonely and desperate that I chose to continue the relationship regardless. Although I was fooling myself, I didn't want to admit it—not to Dr. Harris and not to myself. I remember Dr. Harris telling me that if I didn't stop messing around with married men, I was going to end up in Western State Hospital. But I didn't want to stop seeing this lying jerk so I chose to ignore Dr. Harris' advice. *Oh yes, I was definitely crazy. Webster's New World Dictionary defines crazy as "mentally unbalanced"; and at the time, I was indeed mentally unbalanced.*

Dr. Harris was even kind enough to send me a handwritten note after not hearing from me for some time, simply stating that since it appeared I no longer wanted to continue therapy with him, he hoped I had found a qualified psychiatrist with whom I was working.

So why did I continue to see Greg? I suppose in part because he *seemed* to have my best interests in mind; I was so plain desperate that I would have trusted just about anyone who kept telling me I'd get better. In actuality, I was in such a state of confusion and despair that I was incapable of making any good judgments about much of anything.

I realized I had to do something about Darin. I couldn't care for him in my current condition. It was almost time for school to begin and I was in the pit of despair. I suggested to Greg that maybe Darin should go live with his father until I was better. I simply wanted to be sure that no matter what, Darin would be taken care of.

Greg, for reasons I will never understand or forgive, told me that I had to sign over *complete legal custody* of my son to his father and his wife. Mark had already told his next-door neighbor—who'd also been a friend of mine for years—that he was willing to let Darin live with him until I was well; but oh, no, Greg told me that it had to be done legally "so Darin could *bond* with Mark and Jean. He himself contacted Mark and his wife and set up a meeting with all of us, including my son. This man decided on his own, that I should sign legal documents, in my completely irrational state, giving up complete custody of my son who was the only reason I was still alive!

Even Darin's father, when he walked into Greg's waiting room for our first meeting, and was reading the documents hanging on his wall, turned to me and commented, "Are you sure this guy is qualified and knows what he's doing?" *Hell, no. I'm just desperate enough to trust almost anyone.*

I had no clue if Greg knew what he was doing. I didn't even know what I was doing! This man, calling himself a therapist, actually played lawyer right up to how much child support I should pay! If I'm correct, there are client/patient confidentially laws preventing a person from speaking to anyone else regarding the person they are treating without written consent. At the very minimum, it's highly unethical. Following this first meeting, I took the legal documents drawn up by Mark's wife (who just happened to work in Family Law) to my own attorney. He advised me not to sign *anything* in my current condition that would greatly impact both my life and my son's. He said he'd known me for a long time and that I had in the past been a strong person and that he was sure I would be again.

As I left his office, my ex-husband was standing in the lobby and threatened that if I didn't sign the papers his wife had drawn up, they'd take me to court and have me declared unfit. He reminded me they'd been taking notes on my bizarre behavior, my hospitalizations, and my suicidal threats over the past year or so; and he was sure they would win.

I was so completely terrified of what Mark and Jean might be able to do to me that at our second meeting in Greg's office, I signed the agreement. Laura warned me previously not to sign anything; she begged me to let her go with me to this meeting because she knew what condition I was in and that I'd get screwed; but I told her I could handle it. *I got screwe*d.

My son's welfare was paramount to anything else and I truly did try to put his best interests above my own. I was aware I was in no shape to be making life-altering decisions. So what compelled me to do it? Because I was afraid. Afraid of never being well. Afraid that if didn't sign, and Mark and Jean did take me to court and get custody against my will, I might not even get to see Darin at all. I didn't have the strength or ability to fight back. I couldn't even think straight.

In addition to having no real credentials to even be "treating" me—or anyone else for that matter—for severe depression, Greg had no legal right whatsoever to act as arbitrator in a legal matter affecting the rest of people's lives! I only wish now that the statute of limitations hadn't run out and I could sue. What he did was just plain wrong.

Does anyone believe that a sane person would continue therapy with, and trust someone who had just convinced her to give up legal custody of her son; and in addition, pay child support? That in itself should have qualified me as incompetent to enter into a legal agreement of any kind. Hindsight sucks.

Greg's advice was for me to go home and "feel my pain," stay off the phone, talk to no one, just be alone and "feel my pain" until it went away. He promised me that it would. So that's what I did. I sat in my house, alone, day after day, "feeling my pain" and waiting for it to go away. But it didn't go away. I remember thinking that maybe I wasn't suffering enough even though it felt akin to having my skin peeled off. When would I be through "feeling the pain?" I continued to spiral further and further downward. I tried so hard to believe that what Greg told me was true, that the awful abyss I lived in would end. But it didn't.

Over the course of the next year, my moods fluctuated wildly. At times I was functional; most times I wasn't. I couldn't remember the person I used to be, couldn't believe I'd ever feel normal again.

I tried desperately to keep believing that Greg knew something· I didn't, that he was right, but I continued to be more and more frightened and began to question whether Greg knew what he was doing. *About time, you think?* He was the only person who kept telling me I'd get well. Of course, I was *paying him* not to abandon me, as it seemed everyone else had done, and it was the only hope I felt I had! If he couldn't help me, then I was certainly doomed to living out my life in the darkness of depression as long as I couldn't muster up the courage to kill myself.

I continued to see him, twice a week now; and I begged him to call me once a day, just for five minutes. All I did in our "sessions" was sit in his office and cry and ask him how much longer I had to endure this. He told me he didn't know how long, but that it would happen. It never happened. No matter how much time I spent sitting alone in the pit of despair week after week, nothing changed. I was able to get out of bed each day, shower and dress, and wait. For what?

By the 24th of July 1992, I didn't think I could go through one more minute of this incomprehensible malady. I sat on my bathroom floor with a loaded .38 in my mouth. I was fairly certain a .38 would accomplish the deed. But what if the gun recoiled and I missed? I so wanted to pull the trigger. I just wanted to stop the feelings. But I couldn't bring myself to do it. I just couldn't.

I got in my car and drove myself to the University of Washington Medical Center with the loaded gun in the trunk of my car. I was running out of psychiatric wards. I checked myself into their psychiatric unit. I confessed that I had a loaded .38 in the trunk of my car. I was always honest. Remember the psychiatric hospital in Kirkland? In the psych ward at the University of Washington, I wasn't put in lockup and left there by myself; I wasn't asked if I could afford to pay for my stay; and I saw someone immediately. I was treated as a human being in a great deal of emotional pain who admitted being suicidal. And I wasn't assigned the doctor from hell.

As a contact, I gave them Laura's name and phone number. They called her, she drove over and per their request, removed the gun from my trunk and took it home and put it somewhere safe. I kept thinking there had to be some magic pill, some miracle that could make me well again. All I ever wanted was to be well. After 5 days I was released.

July 29, 1992
Checked out of the hospital yesterday. I am still very depressed, very frightened, barely functioning,

not eating, not sleeping, worried about Darin. Saw Greg for an hour. I'm waiting until 5:00 to see him again. He keeps telling me I have to feel this pain— it's the only way I'll get better. I really hope he knows what he's doing. I can't continue much longer. Nothing in life matters now except being normal again. Nothing helps. Nothing and no one. Even writing doesn't help anymore. I feel like my skin is being peeled off in layers. I am in complete agony. And my son is gone forever.

The first part of September, Greg told me about a place in Arizona that might be able to help me. It was called "Cottonwood" and it would cost me $10,000 for four weeks. He asked if I thought Jacob might pay for it. *Yeah right, that'll happen.* When I called Jacob, he was not happy that this place I wanted to go was in Tucson where he was, and obviously worried that I might try to see him. *And he pay for it? Get real.*

I called Cottonwood myself, talked them into letting me stay for 3 weeks instead of 4, and made arrangements to go. It was my last hope. I spent 3 weeks there, digging into my past, talking about my sexual abuse as a child, reliving old hurts, discussing my father's abandonment, hitting punching bags and beating old mattresses with a tennis racket. I did everything they believed would help. And it did help. It didn't cure my depression, but at least I made peace with a part of my life that caused me a lot of pain. I began to function a little better, a little bit at a time. At the same time, I started on Nardil™ again. It had worked for me a few years back so the doctor on staff thought we'd give it another try.

I called Darin from Cottonwood and tried to explain what was going on but I didn't know how. How could he possibly understand? I didn't completely understand myself. His mother had been in three hospitals for depression and now he was living with his father. I felt so awful about what he must be thinking and feeling.

About the second week I was at Cottonwood, I started to feel better. I will never know if it was the medication, or if my depression had simply reached the end of its cycle. At the end of three weeks I returned home full of hope again of getting my life back together. I was desperately sorry I had agreed to give up legal custody of my son but it was done and all I could do now was try to be the best mom I could be while Darin lived with his father. I found a job and started to work.

Toward the end of October 1992, I met Michael, my husband of 13 years. He'd just been through an awful divorce, was fairly new to Seattle, and was raising a teenage son. Very slowly, we got to know each other and found we had a lot in common. *Except that I was crazy and he wasn't.* I eventually took the chance of telling him about my depressive illness, my hospitalizations, and my marriages. He didn't bolt for the nearest exit; that was a positive. He made me laugh, helped me feel good about myself, and most important, he didn't judge me. We slowly developed a loving and long-lasting relationship that has endured unbelievable odds.

While Michael and I were at his house one evening, I fell and broke my wrist. When he drove me to the nearest hospital, I told them I was taking Nardil® therefore could not be given Demerol® so they gave me morphine for the pain. The next day, after having my wrist put in a cast, I woke up to find my fingers were like giant sausages that looked as if they were going to burst. I was in so much pain that Michael cut the cast a bit to ease the pressure and then drove me back to the hospital. I reminded them of my medications, but apparently no one listened, and they gave me a shot of Demerol®. Giving Demerol® to someone on an MAO inhibitor is tantamount to writing a death sentence. I really thought I was dying. My blood pressure was way off the charts and it's a miracle I survived. Mike told me later than a couple of the nurses were laughing because I thought I was dying, and I only had a broken wrist. Since I didn't die, I couldn't file a lawsuit for medical malpractice. You do not give a patient on an MAOI Demerol®. Ever!

On December 1st, my mother called in the middle of the night to tell me my sister just died of an overdose of sleeping pills. *Seems like there was more than one person in this family with pretty severe problems. Ya think?*

I still grieve my sister's loss but can completely understand how much pain she must have been in, both physically and emotionally, and I understand why it happened. I knew she'd been going through a lot; and I also think she was pretty messed up because of a therapist she was seeing who convinced her she had multiple personality disorder. *Another thing we had in common: an unusual knack for choosing less than ideal therapists.*

This guy wasn't a psychiatrist either—I'm not sure what he was. He even had the gall to call my mother a few days after my sister's death and, without even expressing his sympathy about Lea's death, asked if he could have her diary. Mother said no, read it herself, and then burned it.

I'm so sorry I wasn't there for my sister when she really needed me, but I was so messed up myself that I couldn't begin to help her. Her death devastated my mother. But thank God this happened at a time I was feeling reasonably stable. I took a few days off work and flew to California to help my mother with the funeral arrangements. I think I was mostly numb at the time because I got through it all without a breakdown. My mother really needed me then, and I was glad I could be there for her.

December 29, 1992

Christmas was good. I loved having Darin for a week although I had to work for 3 days while he was here. Mike's been in Colorado with his family and he's called often to profess his undying love for me. So why don't I trust it? How can I trust anyone now?

After Darin went to live with his father and stepmother, Jean started treating me with real contempt. It was painful enough as it was but she made it much harder. She was nasty and rude to me over the phone and God only knows what either Darin's father or stepmother was telling him about me; and there was not one thing I could do about it.

March 14, 1993

Well I faked it through about a 2-week depression without Michael or anyone at work knowing, but I made it.

Darin actually wanted to spend two nights with me; he seems to enjoy the time with Mike's son Todd, and his daughter, Devon. I truly love my son, and his happiness is so damn important to me whether he lives with his father and evil stepmother, or with Mike and me. I just want him to be happy. He's a great kid and I'm proud of him and have told him so. I would really, really give my life for him.

Michael was offered a job in Chicago that promised to be a better position and a good career move. He asked me if I'd consider moving with him and his son. I wanted to be with him but I didn't want to leave Darin. I talked it over with Darin and asked if he'd consider moving with us. Understandably he was comfortable where he was, tired of moving, and I'm sure more than a little worried about his mother's stability after all he'd been through. In addition, his father and stepmother urged him not to go. I can only guess at what all they told him.

That's yet another terrible effect of depressive illness—not only is it life-altering for the person going through it—it also deeply affects those closest to you. Although he didn't talk about it then, I know it impacted his life profoundly.

After a great deal of thought, I made the decision to move with Michael to Illinois. For years after, I berated myself—not only over leaving Darin in Washington—but of what I perceived I'd done to him because of something over which I had no control but

felt responsible for nonetheless. It's taken me years—
and a lot of therapy—to forgive myself.

Following our move to Illinois I began to journal
again, trying to find a pattern and a reason for the
depressions that continued to haunt me. I perused
books on the subject, reading everything I could get
my hands on, amassing a small library of my own.
The depressions continued. They seemed to come
more often, last longer, and they were always severe.
Michael was always there for me and unbelievably
supportive. I was possessed with finding a solution,
going so far as writing to, then calling a psychiatrist
in New York City who had authored one of the many
books I'd read. I spoke to his office about the
possibility of flying to New York to see him for an
evaluation. If I could find someone, anyone, who I
believed could help, I would have gone anywhere!

February 20, 1994

*There are supposedly millions of us out there
living with this illness. I wouldn't be the first to take
my own life, and not the last. I don't want to die just
as I believe most others don't really want to die. I
just want to stop the pain. I don't know how to stop
the pain. I've tried medication, I've tried hospitalization,
I've tried prayer, I've tried a $10,000 program in
Tucson. I've even tried Greg's ridiculous advice to
"sit at home doing nothing but feel the pain." That*

one cost me my son and $600 a month in child support. Am I bitter? You bet I am. Am I angry? Big time. Am I tired of fighting? Definitely. Am I ready to give up? I don't know, sometimes I think I can't take one more day and then I think, "What if I killed myself and they found a cure?"

I am not weak. I am not crazy. This is not anyone's fault. It's an evil force that I have fought for years; one that at times I thought had been conquered, or at least managed. But what the psychiatrists, the psychologists, the faith healers, the scientists, the drug companies, the people who've never actually FELT what this is like don't understand is that NO MATTER HOW MUCH TENACITY, NO MATTER HOW MUCH DETER-MINATION, NO MATTER HOW MUCH ONE'S CAPACITY FOR PAIN IS, THERE COMES A TIME THAT YOU SIMPLY CAN'T FIGHT IT ANYMORE. YOU GIVE UP! YOU LOSE ALL HOPE! You die inside so completely that you're not even living anymore. NO ONE could possibly understand this illness unless they've LIVED IT - NO ONE!

From June of 1994 through most of December I was definitely in a remission. I changed medications a few times during that period so I have absolutely no clue whether the medication helped or the depression simply reached the end of its cycle.

Michael and I were married in Cancun, Mexico, on November 11, 1994. He is my best friend. He has stood by me through all this as no one else could. He has been my rock. He has held me when I was in so much pain I could only cry. It's not easy living with someone with wildly fluctuating mood swings. I wonder sometimes why he loves me so much. I've finally dealt with the "if he loves me there must be something wrong with him" conflict. I love him with all my heart. I finally know what unconditional love is and I'm able to return it.

Near the end of December the depression was back. December and the first half of January were awful. Because I wasn't getting any better no matter what medications I was on, the first part of January, Michael and I talked it over with my psychiatrist and we decided that I would try ECT—formerly known as shock treatments. I agreed to it because at the time, it was either that or suicide.

A series of ECT usually consists of six to twelve treatments, although the patient may decline to have that many. Treatments can be administered to either inpatients or outpatients.

Medications are induced intravenously to relax the muscles of the body and to reduce saliva. The patient is put to sleep with general anesthesia. During ECT, an amount of electricity is sent to the non-dominant side (unilateral) or both sides (bilateral) of the brain via electrodes attached to the head. This current produces brain wave (EEG) changes that are characteristic of a grand mal seizure that affects the entire brain, including the parts that control mood, appetite, and sleep. Although it is not known precisely how ECT works, it is believed to correct biochemical abnormalities that may underlie the psychiatric condition.

Beginning January 13 and ending January 20, I had four ECT treatments. The doctor administering them performed them bilaterally (meaning the electrodes were placed on both sides of my temples rather than just one side). Some doctors believe that bilateral treatments produce quicker, more effective results. It also causes, as it did in my case, more short-term memory loss and confusion. I would not remember much of the following had I not kept a journal because I have very little cognitive recollection of the events around that time.

January 22, 1995

Made arrangements to meet Carol at a movie. I left in my car but forgot where I was going and what I was doing. I ended up stopping at Olive Garden and having lunch by myself. Then I got lost driving home—several times. It was as if I was in a different world or was a different person. When I got home,

Carol called and asked me why I didn't show up. I'd completely forgotten about meeting her!
January 24, 1995
I tried to go to work but got lost and finally arrived at 11:00 a.m. I couldn't remember how to work the computer and I basically sat in front of it all day just looking at it. I didn't feel "crazy" like the day before, but I was behaving very strangely. The people at work kept asking me if I was OK.

January 25, 1995
Woke up feeling totally out of it, as if I was on some mind-altering drug. I had no control of what I was thinking—couldn't discern reality from un-reality, had no concept of time. I stayed in bed all day—not because of depression this time—because of confusion and sickness. I never got dressed. I vomited. I called Michael at work several times during the day in terror. Each time I called he told me I'd just called 5 minutes before. I didn't know that. I wouldn't make it without Michael. He is truly my best friend. I didn't think I should be feeling this way, didn't think what I was experiencing was normal. He told me to call Dale at the hospital where I had the ECT, and Dale would tell me it was normal. I called and he wasn't there. The person I did talk to told me that my last treatment was more than five days ago so what I was experiencing could have

*nothing to do with the ECT. That really panicked me.
I took 5 mg of Valium three times just to calm down. I
was really, really afraid I was losing my mind.*

January 26, 1995

I called Dale at the hospital again and told him
what they had told me when I tried to call him on
Monday. He said they were wrong and asked who I
had talked to. I didn't know.

January 27, 1995

*I feel much better, less confused, more in control.
I called Dale again because I was beginning to
remember how scared I was on Monday. He changed
his story from the day before. He now tells me that
the feeling of being crazy and out of control is not
related to the ECT. I suppose someone there spoke
with him. That really terrified me! I've had four ECT
treatments in the past two weeks. I haven't been
depressed, but not matter what the hospital tells me, I
know I've had a reaction to the ECT.*

*Once I realized that my panic and fear of insanity
really are a side effect of the ECT, I was able to calm
down and am beginning to get a grip on reality. I'm
still a little confused from time to time but at least I
know I have a valid reason. It's a side effect of the
ECT; it has to be, regardless of what they tell me.
They're just trying to protect themselves; I've never*

ever in my life felt these kinds of crazy things until after it. I don't want to die anymore. I want to live. My only concern now is to be sane. I'm not worried about depression right now. I'm worried about my sanity.

January 29, 1995

Got up at 4:30 a.m., had 3 cups of coffee, felt great but wired! Started to feel a little frightened until I ate some food and then I began to calm down and was OK the rest of the day. Flew to Seattle.

January 30, 1995

Felt wonderful all day—no depression, no confusion. Picked up Darin and went to dinner with him and Roger and Marsha. When we got back to their house, Darin said to me, "Mom, are you on some new medication or something?" I replied, "Why, am I acting weird?" I must have given him a strange look because he then said, "Oh, it's OK, Mom. I like you a lot better this way than depressed."

This was my first experience with hypomania. It was the most wonderful feeling imaginable. I was euphoric, talked faster than I could think, needed very little sleep, and I was in love with the whole world. After months and months of the most wrenching, awful, suicidal depression, I thought I was cured! It was over!

Many of us who've experienced hypomania (literally, mild mania) wish we could maintain that state of ultimate bliss; but alas, cycling back and forth between depression and hypomania or mania is the nature of the beast. It's called bipolar disorder—a newer name for manic depression. Having bipolar disorder rather than unipolar (meaning experiencing only the debilitating lows on the one end of the axis [or pole] without shifting to the other end—the euphoria) might seem the better alternative; but take it from someone who's been there, it isn't. The highs don't even begin to make up for the crushing lows.

For those who don't know, let me try to more clearly explain the difference between unipolar depression and bipolar disorder. Unipolar depression, also known as clinical, or major depression, applies to those individuals who experience episodes of depression, but not its opposite: mania.

Bipolar disorder is an illness that causes extreme mood changes that *alternate* between major depression and mania. The mood changes of bipolar disorder can be mild or extreme. They may develop gradually over several days or weeks, or come on suddenly within minutes or hours. Either the manic or depressive episodes may only last a few hours or for several months. And to make it even more confusing, there are two basic types of mania: euphoric and dysphoric. A person can experience both types.

With euphoria, a person is high, in love with the world, feels boundless energy, talks a mile a minute, mind is racing, deluded with grandiose thoughts, spends money without thought of consequence, takes unreasonable risks. He loses most feelings of responsibility. This kind of mania is usually the kind described in the popular literature.

As with euphoria, a person in *dysphoric* mania can also exhibit the above symptoms. However, in dysphoric mania, the person is still "high" but in a different sense: agitated, destructive, full of rage, paranoid, full of anxiety, panic-stricken. Full-blown mania may be sufficiently severe to cause impairment in social or occupational functioning or to require hospitalization, or it can be characterized by the presence of psychotic features.

And if you're really lucky, as I was, you can experience hypomania. With hypomania, the symptoms are basically the same but less severe— inflated self-esteem but at a level of uncritical self-confidence rather than grandiosity, still a decreased need for sleep—waking up after only a few hours with increased energy. However, hypomania is not severe enough to be classified as full-blown mania.

Several studies have shown that those with bipolar illness usually experience their first episode of either depression or mania in their early to mid-20s, which is when I experienced my first major depression. In some cases, bipolars have mostly manic cycles with few, and occasionally, no depressive cycles. Sometimes a depressive episode will occur much later, after many manic episodes.

Other times, as I believe it was in my case, the opposite will occur: many depressive cycles and only a few manic (or hypomanic).

From the books and articles I've read regarding this, one of the explanations is that you can cycle in and out of depressive cycles and never experience hypomanic (or manic) cycles, yet still be considered bipolar because of the frequency and rapidity of the depressive cycles. If the varying types of bipolar disorder aren't confusing enough, dysphoria can occur along *with* depression. These are referred to as "mixed episodes."

After years of misdiagnosis, I was eventually diagnosed as bipolar II, rapid-cycling. It doesn't get much better than that.

One day when I was feeling particularly desperate, I decided to go buy another gun. By then, we had two .38s that Mike had locked in a safe so I wouldn't have access to them. On my way to the gun shop, I pulled off the road and dug through my purse searching for the names and phone numbers of a couple of therapists I had gotten from the church we'd been attending. The first one I called didn't answer. The second one did. I was sobbing and I told her I was on my way to buy a gun to kill myself with. She told me to come to her office right then and talked to me on my cell phone as I drove there. This happened on a Friday and although I didn't know it then, Lois didn't normally work on Fridays; she just happened to be in her office that day doing paperwork. I arrived at her office, went in and between sobs, managed to tell her as much as I could about all the years of depression and the hopelessness that was so prevalent.

I saw Lois many times after that. She is a loving, caring person who actually liked me in spite of my depression. With her, I could vent my fear, my suicidal thoughts—everything—and she listened. She asked questions; we talked about options, about faith, about everything. She wasn't able to cure my depressions but there were times she kept me from suicide just by being there when I needed her. Even after we moved from Illinois, I stayed in touch with her via the phone; she even called me a few times to see how I was doing. I love this woman and her support has been invaluable in helping me to hang in there many times when I didn't believe I could.

Due to a lot of back pain I'd been experiencing, and after canceling my first scheduled surgery due to the depression I was then experiencing, I finally agreed to go ahead with it, reasoning I could always kill myself later. *Maybe I'd even be lucky enough to die in surgery.* I was still very depressed when I went in for my surgery. On September 18, I had a laminectomy on the lumbar portion of my spine. The surgery took four hours. I woke up the next day the hospital and felt like the depression was gone. I felt great. The next day I went home; and the morning after I was up at four o'clock ironing. I couldn't sleep and felt wonderful.

I have since read, in my personal quest for information, that sometimes after anesthesia, the anesthesia itself can have a positive effect on a person's mood and can actually reverse the mood from one of depression. For several weeks following my surgery, I felt wonderful, with some hypomanic symptoms. However, it seems only a certain type of anesthesia produces that effect. Unfortunately, which type of anesthesia that is, I don't know.

Over time I've come to develop a healthy degree of self-esteem in spite of my bipolar illness. I like myself. The fear that people will find out I have bipolar disorder and subsequently judge me as though it were somehow my fault is no longer there. OK, so a great many people still don't understand what major depression is. Not my fault. I'm no longer ashamed to admit it. If someone makes a judgment of me as a person because I have what many perceive to be a mental illness, then they aren't worth my time anyway.

When I decided to try and write a book about my experience, I was at first too insecure and afraid to admit what I was writing. Now when I'm having a conversation with someone and the subject comes up that I'm writing a book and I'm asked, "What's your book about? Is it fiction?" I'm able to say without shame or fear of scaring someone away, "It's about my experience with bipolar disorder." This is a big step for me, being secure enough in myself that should someone choose to judge me because I'm bipolar, it's their problem, not mine. What's most amazing is that since I've reached this point, most people are encouraging and even proud of me for daring to take this on.

Still, even after sharing some of my writing with people who've known me for years, a few have asked, "What is bipolar?" Or, "When I told my mother you were writing a book about your depression, she wanted to know how you could possibly be depressed—you have a great husband, a beautiful home, you're attractive, you're smart—why would you be depressed?" Some people still don't get it.

Michael and I moved to Denver in June of 1997. I was fine throughout the move and for several weeks after. Then, zap, back down in the black hole. This one lasted an eternity. *Don't they all?* I managed to find a psychiatrist in Denver who I really liked, but alas, none of the new, improved antidepressants worked; thus in the later part of August, I agreed to another round of ECT provided they would do unilateral only because of my bad experience with bilateral the first time around. Recall that *unilateral* involves placing the electrodes that deliver the "shock" on one side of the head only, whereas *bilateral* involves placing the electrodes on both sides.

After four treatments with no measurable improvement, my doctor talked me into agreeing to two more. Because she thought bilateral was more effective, she convinced me to go that route. On September 3, I was awake all night and definitely into hypomanic mode. Although I was obviously no longer depressed, my doctor urged me to have at least one more treatment on the 6th of September, again bilateral.

After those six treatments, my mood remained good but I became very confused and frightened, so much so that that I couldn't go to sleep and started to panic. I felt much like I had following the first series of treatments two years before and frankly, it scared the hell out of me. I couldn't remember which night I had become hypomanic; I couldn't remember what I did the week before. I remember seeing Princess Diana all over the news because she'd been killed the night before, but it barely registered at the time. It was like a dream.

I wonder if perhaps the confusion and fear might have been due to switching to the bilateral treatments, or if it would have occurred anyway. Interesting to note, however, after having three unilateral treatments, I switched to a hypomanic phase without going through the confusion, fear, or memory loss.

While we were living in Denver, I was so desperate for a cure I tried everything, even going so far as—after reading a book on demonic oppression and Christians—finding a minister in Colorado who dealt in demonic exorcisms. *Is it becoming clear how desperate I was?* Not wanting to leave any stone unturned, I convinced Michael to accompany me to see this man. It was worth the hundred dollars he charged to at least find out that I wasn't possessed with a demon. That was a relief. One less thing to worry about.

I still don't understand how, when my body chemistry is "normal," life is mostly good. But when that same chemistry gets out of whack, everything that once seemed good suddenly looks bleak and hopeless. I can't explain it, the psychiatrists can't explain it, it just happens.

In September of 1997, Darin came to visit before starting college and it was wonderful to see him. While he was visiting, I asked him to read the portion of my book that I had written in the hope that he would be able to better understand why I gave up custody of him, why my behavior was so bizarre during that time, and what depressive illness really is. At the airport, just as he was boarding the plane to fly home to Seattle, he handed me a note he had written. It read:

"Dear Mom, I just want to say that I love you and I will always be there for you. I have never completely understood your depression but the book you are writing has helped me begin to understand. I am sorry for my ignorance. I love you always. Your son."

It was the most beautiful, meaningful thing I'd ever read. I sat down in the waiting area and cried for 10 minutes. It meant the world to me. It was a breakthrough. He had begun to understand. It was no longer an ugly black secret. He could accept me even with my illness; he loved me as I was.

In the years that have since passed, my son and I have established a wonderful relationship. I am incredibly proud of him and his accomplishments; and I know he is proud of mine.

When talking with other people about his children, Michael refers to Darin as one of his own kids, yet in no way tries to replace or demean his biological father. Darin is my pride and joy. Telling me how proud he is of my tenacity, my inner strength, and my ability to never give up has made a profound difference in alleviating the guilt I carried far too long.

Those who have never experienced a mood disorder have no conception of how fortunate they are. How could they? For them, life is on a fairly even keel. Sure, they have their normal ups and downs but they don't know what it's like to have an *illness* like depression. The brain is a fascinating organ. If even one little thing, one tiny neuron can't connect to its receptor for some reason or other, it can cause suffering beyond the imagination.

Can you imagine what it's like to go through the motions of living and not feel anything—not just for a couple of days, but for months at a time? Can you imagine waking up every morning terrified of something you can't even identify? Can you imagine what it's like to have no hope for any joy throughout the day? Can you imagine what it's like to look at yourself in the mirror and hate what you see just because you hate everything right now? Can you imagine what it's like to believe that no matter how tenacious you are, how strong, it's never going to change—you're always going to have this damn depression?

The first week in October, I started to feel depressed again. It's like living on an emotional roller coaster! I was depressed the whole month of October—another great birthday. I was working the month of September and continued to work through October, even though I was horribly depressed. Working did give me a reason to get up in the morning and a place to go and, amazingly, I functioned while I was working. I was able to pretend I was OK while I was there. I didn't feel OK, and I wasn't my usual lighthearted, always kidding around, outgoing self—which I am when not depressed—but I faked it pretty well.

October 25, 1997

I can't decide whether to live or die. Suicide is a constant thought. All day I think about getting in my car with a couple bottles of Valium and driving up into the mountains, taking the Valium and hoping to freeze to death. I just don't know. I think I want to end my life. I think about it so much, it's constantly on my mind. But then there's always something that stops me. What? Is it a fear that I won't know how Darin's life turns out. Is it a fear of something else? I still don't want to hurt Darin, God knows. Suicide is such an ugly thing to do to your family. But it would stop this horrible pain! I can't even write decently anymore. I'm writing like a 4th grader. I've lost it. I'm on the edge. Can I push myself on over? I don't know.

Back in the pit of darkness the first of November, I stayed on the sofa most of the day, sleeping off and on. Then one night when we were getting ready to go to bed, I said to Michael, "You know, when I go from a depressive phase into a hypomanic phase, I am always up the entire night, wired. I wonder what would happen if I just forced myself to stay up all night." So I decided to try it. What did I have to lose?

I wrote. I read. I played computer games. I paid bills. The longer I stayed up, the better I felt. By 5:00 the next morning, I felt wonderful. I went to the grocery store at 6:00 a.m. We went to church at 9:00. I stayed up the entire day so I would be able to sleep that night. I was tired but I wasn't sleepy. I went to bed about 7:00 p.m.

At the time I came upon this new "treatment," I'd never heard of using sleep deprivation to bring about a mood swing. In fact, when I mentioned it to my psychiatrist, she'd not yet heard anything about using sleep deprivation to switch out of a depressive cycle. When I told my mother-in-law what I'd done and how it had worked, she got all excited and wanted me to hurry up and finish my book; she said maybe I'd discovered a new cure. *I wish.*

I started searching for information on sleep deprivation and came across articles written on using sleep deprivation as a means of modifying sleep patterns in depressed patients, called *resetting the biological clock,* and it has been successful to some degree. Studies indicate that patients who have undergone this resetting find relief but periodically have to repeat the procedure. Studies on sleep patterns of bipolar patients are amazingly contradictory, but it is widely accepted that total sleep deprivation and partial sleep deprivation in the second half of the night can bring about temporary remissions in unipolar and bipolar patients in their depressed state.

It seems to be the timing of the sleep deprivation that correlates with improvement. Losing four hours of sleep in the first half of the night does not make a difference; losing it in the second half of the night or advancing the entire sleep period by six hours can reduce or eliminate depression.

Also, it seems to do with stages of sleep that are marked by the presence or absence of REM (rapid eye movement). Most people go through progressively deeper stages of a non-REM period when blood pressure and heart rate slow down, muscles relax, and the eyes are still. Then they go through REM sleep, the period when pulse and blood pressure rise and fall. It is at this time that we dream and our mental activity speeds up. REM sleep is usually most concentrated just before waking up. Interrupting REM sleep, in some mysterious way, seems to short-circuit depression. However, sleep deprivation for someone who has bipolar illness is risky, doctor's caution, because it can precipitate mania.

On the other hand, I seem to fall immediately into REM sleep without going through the non-REM stage. Why do I think this? Because even when I fall asleep for 30 minutes, I dream, and usually remember the dream. I seem to dream immediately after falling asleep on a regular basis. Could it be that I get too much REM sleep, and not enough non-REM sleep? Could it be that in patients in which sleep deprivation works, this the case? Too much REM sleep and no enough of the other?

I was thrilled that it worked! I couldn't believe it. I told my family, "I don't know how long it will last but I'm feeling good again." With bipolar illness you can only take one day at a time, and you're thankful for the good days and only pray that they last. I was definitely hypomanic for almost three weeks. When depression is followed by hypomania, it's wonderful. I did all the things I hadn't felt like doing when I was depressed. I cleaned house from top to bottom, I paid bills, I cooked again, I shopped, and I saw friends I hadn't felt like seeing in a long time.

By the 21st of November, I started feeling really irritable and crabby. Sometimes that's how I know another depressive episode is just around the corner—I start out feeling really irritable and angry. I was not working at this time so I just lay around the house all day, played computer games and watched TV. I didn't feel like doing anything but I wasn't flat-on-my-back depressed.

When the temp agency called me about a job, I decided to take it just to have something to keep me busy. I would wake up in the mornings not wanting to get out of bed, but forced myself to, went to work; and while at work, I functioned. I was for the most part, cheerful and productive but when I came home at night, I didn't want to cook, or eat, or do anything except watch TV. I didn't feel like Christmas shopping although I needed to. I kept telling myself I'd do it next week or next week, or whatever. I wanted to try the sleep deprivation again but I was afraid it wouldn't work, or if it did, that it wouldn't last through Christmas, and all the kids were coming for Christmas—Darin, Mike's daughter Devon from Wisconsin, and Mike's son Todd, who lived in

Denver. I wanted so much for it to be a happy Christmas, to be able to enjoy it; and for Darin to see me happy.

Twice I tried staying up all night. The first time I made it till 5:00 a.m. and was so exhausted I went to bed and slept till 8:00 a.m. I was still depressed. The second time I made it till 1:00 a.m. I was still depressed. December 20, I tried it again. This time I forced myself to stay up. I started to feel better early in the morning although I was very tired. I managed to make it through the next day and slept well that night. By the grace of God, I felt good through Christmas.

It didn't last .From the first part of January through the middle of February, I went from the depths to ok, then back to the depths. I tried the sleep deprivation five times in January and February. Twice I had no success; three times it brought me back up, but only for two weeks, and then I crashed again. I don't understand why it worked some times and not others. I've come to the conclusion that it might have something to do with the time in between—the longer I waited to stay up all night, the better the results. This is not scientific fact; I couldn't figure it out.

March 10, 1999

What can I do? I know I shouldn't be sitting here thinking about suicide. I don't want to hurt anyone.

But I'm giving up. I've tried everything—medications, ECT, sleep deprivation, cognitive therapy, you name it. If there's something out there I haven't tried, then someone's keeping it from me. I've tried to have faith; I've struggled with it for years now. I feel so useless, so empty.

I get up in the morning, shower and spend the day playing computer games, watching TV, or reading, anything to keep me from thinking. I'm alive but I'm not living. I exist. I have all the blinds drawn. I don't want to have to talk to anyone. I don't even want to go out. I'm afraid someone will see me, look at me and know that I'm just not there.

People love me. Mike loves me. Darin loves me. That's not the problem. The problem is the illness. When the depression hits, it wipes out all hope, all faith, all feeling. I'm losing the battle. Mike tells me "You'll get through this, just hang in there". God, I've been "hanging in there" for how many years? I've written about all this shit a hundred times and the tune and the words are still the same. It's useless to keep on saying it over and over because it never changes. I feel good for a while and then it comes back—it always comes back. I'm a mole. I bury myself and I exist. That's it. I exist. If I don't make it through this one, then please, please understand that I just ran out of strength. I'm sorry. It's not anyone's fault. It's not even my fault. It's the fucking illness' fault.

July 24, 1999

It's as if I'm looking back at another life, another person. I remember what it felt like to feel happy; but I can't quite grasp it. I can almost see it. Picture it. Taste it. But it's just a movie I'm watching; it's not the real thing anymore. Why can't I shake it, talk myself out of it? Sometimes I think maybe I can. It's just a matter of strength. I know I'm strong. Look at all I've been through and survived.

I'm so worried about Darin. I just pray that he never feels this kind of hurt. I know it will go away, or at least I'm pretty sure it will. It always has. I remember that each time I go through a depression, I always think that maybe this is the time it won't go away. That it will just hang on until I simply can't take another minute of it and I'll finally do myself in. But that's silly. I could never do that. Think of how it would affect Darin. He needs me now more than he ever has. He needs to know that no matter what I've been through, I'm strong enough to hang on. He needs to know that if he should ever really need me, I'll be there ready to guide him, support him, love him through whatever he has to face. He needs to know that if he should ever get depressed like this, he can count on me to guide him through it. What if I gave up? What would that tell him? Oh God, why am I cursed with this? Why so long? Why does it keep coming back? Why can't it be over?

Sometimes I think it would be so much better to just drive down to the beach at night and wander into the water and let it take me out and end this unbearable pain that I live with. Sometimes I wish I could do it. Life's gone on too long for me...other people want to live to old age but not me. I've lived long enough. Depression is always just around the corner, lying in wait—menacing, ugly, evil. Just waiting to rip me apart one more time, see if it can tear me into little pieces so small that I can't put them back together again. I hate it. I hate this disease.

Instead of the death penalty, they should have the depression penalty. There should be some kind of injection that you could give criminals that would induce major clinical depression. That'd take care of them. We wouldn't have to put them to death. Just put them in major depression. They'd be perfectly harmless except to themselves. Besides, I can't think of a more horrid punishment for anyone that to condemn someone to major depression for the rest of his life. It's surely worse than death. At least with death, it's over. I like to think of death as an endless sleep. There's no pain in sleep. That's what people who kill themselves are thinking: Sleep. Endless sleep. No more thinking, no more fear, no more pain. Just sleep.

May 5, 2000

How long can I ride on this highway to hell? After 2-1/2 months of Nightmare on Elm Street, I called my doctor and cried, "HELP." I scheduled ECT. Then I woke up the very next morning and it was gone! Like someone flipped a switch. It was just GONE. It was wonderful. I did laundry, I ironed, I polished silver that was almost black from neglect. I watered plants. I called people and had real conversations. I had a friend over and actually cooked dinner.

Then, on Tuesday, May 2nd, I felt kind of down again. I told myself, "Don't panic, Lora. Everyone feels down sometimes. Doesn't mean you're going back into hell. When a depression ends, you usually have at least a month before it comes back."

And we've had no action on the house. None. So the place we wanted to buy in Westchester, Illinois, is no longer available. They couldn't hold it forever. We'll have to start looking all over again. And I miss my husband. I haven't seen him in two weeks. It gets expensive flying home every weekend, even with the company paying 1/2 the fare. He's coming home tomorrow night. Then back to Chicago on Monday morning. If I were OK, I wouldn't mind being alone. Up until Monday the 3rd, I did just fine. But when this black fog descends, nothing makes sense. All I can do is live one day at a time, and keep praying to a God I don't understand. Even though I know it's not my fault, it doesn't help. I still feel like a loser. I still feel like someone who has a "mental illness." I know that *people are tired of hearing, "Lora's not doing so well again."*

This time it lasted 2-1/2 months. The depression. That's longer than it's lasted in a very long time. I tried the sleep deprivation therapy about five times during this episode and guess what? It hasn't worked. Big surprise. I've contacted several places doing new clinical trials for new treatments, and so far, nothing. I've been on almost every antidepressant and mood stabilizer on the market and still, I cycle in and out of this no matter what I'm taking.

I don't understand this illness I have. I know a lot about it but I don't understand it. The past 2-1/2 months have been torture. It started the first week in February and ended on April 22. How long can I endure this? There are days when I don't get out of bed at all and days that I do get out of bed but don't shower and dress until late in the day before Michael comes home. Then there are days that I manage to get it together enough to actually do something. I force myself. I never feel good, but there are days I manage to function to some extent. I pretend to be OK so no one will know. I've played tennis, gone to a movie, and even gone to dinner with people when all I really wanted to do was die. But for a few hours, in order to appear normal, I can put on my plastic face, smile, and act as if I'm OK. It takes a lot of energy. I'm pretty sure the people who know about my depressions can see through the facade but those who don't, have no clue. I'm a very good actress— but only for a few hours, then I retreat to the safety of my home, don't answer the phone or the door or even get the mail because then I might have to actually talk to someone and they could tell that I'm not OK.

I cry uncontrollably, feeling like the tears could go on forever. Even worse are the times that I think about how to kill myself. I've gone through every method in my head from overdosing to drowning to shooting myself. I always manage to find a reason not to do it. God, I've been so close. I've held a loaded gun against my head, unable to pull the trigger. Mostly, I think about how it would affect Darin. How could I do such a horrid thing to my son? How would he cope? What would he feel? Who would he turn to if he needed me and I wasn't there? Even knowing about my depressions, could he possibly understand why I couldn't go on one more day?

Going through these cycles is like being two different people: There's the Lora who wakes up afraid of the day ahead, who wants to stay in bed and hide, who won't answer the phone or the door because she's afraid to talk to anyone, who feels totally and completely without hope and thinks constantly of suicide. I don't really want to die; I just don't want to feel like this. It's unbearable.

Then when the fog lifts, there's a whole other person. When a depression ends, it's like somebody flipped a switch. It happens that quickly. After weeks or months of wondering how long I can keep this up, suddenly it's gone.

And then I become a completely different person. I'm happy, love people, enjoy life, paint kitchens and bathrooms, love to shop, enjoy cooking and even entertaining. Both of these people know about the other but the depressed Lora can't believe she'll ever feel good again.

When I'm "up," I can remember how awful the depression was; I ask myself, "What is it that could possibly cause me to feel that kind of hopelessness when right now, I'm OK? Right now I can't comprehend that kind of terror. What possible brain chemistry could cause a person to perceive the world as so completely black? Nothing in my life has changed except my perceptions. How can I change my perceptions? How can I change my brain chemistry? When I'm feeling good, when the depression is in remission, then I have to do everything I couldn't do while I was depressed because I never know how much time I'll have before it comes back.

But the roller coaster that I ride on is ripping my soul apart. I cycle rapidly—sometimes I feel good for a couple of months followed by a month or more of black, hopeless depression. Sometimes the depression will only last a few days. Sometimes I feel good for only a week or two. I never know how far I can plan ahead for anything because I never know where I'll be then—emotionally. Until recently, I always knew that I had at least a month or more before I had to worry about it coming back. This time the remission lasted less than two weeks.

I don't think anyone tries harder than I to find a solution. I've hardly left a stone unturned. I've read every book I could get my hands on. I've searched out web sites for new clinical trials looking for volunteers; I've applied to several. But so far, I've been turned down either because I take synthroid— and they won't take anyone on thyroid medication; or because I'm bipolar and their study wants only unipolar patients; and the one I came closest to getting into finally turned me down because they said I cycle too rapidly. What does a person do to continue to struggle to survive when there appears to be very little hope of ever being well? Can anyone blame those who feel as if they've tried everything and do finally give up and take their lives?

I start a job tomorrow. How the hell can I do that? There are degrees of depression. There are times when I'm depressed but somehow able to function, at least part of the time. I'm able to go through the motions of living, perform the necessary tasks; and other times I'm completely unable to do anything—even get out of bed.

Depressive illness and bipolar disorder are such complicated, ambiguous, portentous illnesses. They affect everything we are, everything we feel and everything we do. And those on the outside have absolutely no comprehension of it, no understanding of what it is to be immersed in its darkness. If they could only comprehend how hard we try. They can read about symptoms, they can study treatments, some can even make diagnoses based on the literature. Some can even look at a person in so much pain and see that they are, indeed, suffering. No one, however, who hasn't *felt* its paralyzing power, can possibly begin to know what it's like to personally experiencing it. That's why we feel so completely isolated.

Christmas 2000 was the worst. Mike and I were having a Christmas party on the 23rd. My son, Darin, and my stepdaughter, Devon, were coming from out of town so I was really looking forward to having a wonderful family Christmas.

We had about 30 people coming for the party and I'd been busy putting up decorations, fixing food, all the things you do for a party. I was feeling great—had been since November 15 after coming out of a 5-1/2 week depression. After finally being diagnosed as Bipolar II Rapid Cycling, I'd been charting my mood cycles since the beginning of 1999. I'm usually afraid to plan anything like a big party because the depressions come so sporadically that I never know when one might hit; but I had been feeling good for nearly a month, a pretty long time for me. I was excited that Darin could see me happy and enjoying myself entertaining.

As I said, the party was the 23rd, the day before Christmas Eve. It was a smashing success. Everyone had a good time. After everyone had gone home, around midnight, I began to sense that familiar creepy feeling setting in. I was definitely feeling down. Scary down. I decided to stay up all night to try and ward off a depression. It had worked many times before, but not this time. The longer I was up the worse I felt. Around 3:00 a.m. I was in panic mode. I knew this one was going to be bad. Why God, why? Why do I have to keep going through this? Why does Christmas have to be spoiled? What have I done to deserve this over and over?

Mike woke up around 4:00 or 4:30 a.m. to find me sitting on the bed wringing my hands and crying. I was near hysterical. We had planned to take the kids to church with us but they were too tired, and I was too messed up to push it. Mike and I went alone. I don't even know how I managed to get dressed. At church I don't remember much about the service except that all I could do was cry. This was supposed to be a great Christmas. I'd even planned what I would say for grace before we had Christmas dinner. I had so much to be thankful for, and I was so glad to have Darin there; I just wanted it to be a great Christmas for everyone. It wasn't.

That evening we were all going to Larry and Suszette's for dinner with their family. As soon as we walked in, I grabbed Suszette and told her I was in bad shape. She and I were close enough that I'd shared with her my problems with depression. She was concerned but the evening went on. I can be a great actress when it comes to hiding my pain from others. I performed. I made it through.

The next day was Christmas Day. Oh my God, I had invited a single friend over for dinner. There was simply no way I could appear normal in front of her. I asked Mike to call her and tell her I had come down with a terrible flu. I couldn't think of any alternative. I couldn't tell her the truth; she was not a person who could possibly understand. She had no conception of major depression.

Operating on autopilot, I got the turkey in the oven. I'd forgotten to buy potatoes. Mike went to the store and bought instant mashed potatoes; it was all he could find on Christmas Day. Somehow I managed to throw the dinner together and we sat down and ate. Or rather, they ate. I had no appetite, but I tried very hard to appear normal. I don't think anyone except Michael had any idea what horrible shape I was in. I simply wanted to not exist.

How I made it through the day, I don't remember. The plan had been for Darin and me to drive the Acura that he was buying from us to Seattle from Chicago the day after Christmas. I was going to fly back to Chicago on New Year's Day. I literally forced myself to get up that morning. Mike didn't want me to do it; he said I was in no shape to handle a drive like that. So I called Darin's father and asked if he would split the cost to ship the car to Seattle. He said absolutely not. *Big surprise.*

I told Mike that I had promised Darin and I couldn't disappoint him; that I could somehow manage. So we loaded up the car and left. Darin had no idea of the condition I was in. I tried the best I could to keep him from knowing. I must have done pretty well because when I finally told him about it, he said he had absolutely no clue. Every morning on the road when I awoke at dawn, I just kept forcing myself to get up and go. To this day, I do not know how I managed to do it, but we somehow made it all the way.

I spent New Year's Eve in a small motel near the airport so I could fly home the next morning. It was, without comparison, the most horrible Christmas and New Year I've ever lived through. Darin didn't know until years later. Why should he have to deal with worrying about me when there was nothing he could have done? At least I could spare him.

Between January of 1995 and August of 2001, I had a total of thirty ECT's. After each series, although they did bring me out of suicidal depression, I needed more treatments to achieve the same result; and each time there was always the confusion, the short-term memory loss, and the out of control feelings before the hypomania began. And the depressions still came back.

I don't believe I'd ever resort to ECT again. I've read of many horror stories of the negative effects; many have claimed complete loss of memory. Conversely, there are also proponents of the treatment who say it's saved their lives. If I was to ever find myself in that suicidal place again, I can't say for sure what I'd do.

For anyone considering it, however, my advice would be to research it very carefully, or have your family do so. If you can, discuss it with others who've been through it. For some it's worked wonders; others haven't been so fortunate.

December 25, 2002

I'm sitting here looking out at the beauty of new fallen snow. I'm oh so grateful that it's been nearly six months since I last had a severe depression. It's as if God has finally smiled upon me and given me a long respite from all the pain of the years before. I pray, "Dear God, please, please never, ever let me fall into that black abyss again." I wonder how I survived all those years of torment, many times wanting so badly to die yet somehow managing to hang on.

At one time, I used to make deals with myself. "Ok, if I can just make it through Darin's H.S. graduation, then I can kill myself." So I did that. Then it was, "Ok, if I can just get him settled in college, then I can do it." Then it was, "Well, now I have to help him move into his apartment." Then it was, "well, let's just see if anyone is really interested in publishing my book." It went on and on and on. I could always find a reason to postpone it. Thank God.

Although I've been very angry with God for allowing me to suffer the way I have, he has brought me through the fire. Without my faith, I know I would not be here now. It's not my intent to preach to anyone; I know there are people who cannot conceive of a God who would allow such suffering. I don't have the answers. I don't know why bad things happen to good people. Just over six years ago, most of my thoughts were consumed with suicide. How I stayed alive and kept fighting, I do not know, except that what faith I still had in God sustained me— barely. I still don't understand why it happens—not just to me but to anyone. I may never know. All I do know is that I truly believe that is God is responsible for where I am now. Even if I'm wrong, I'm not losing anything. I'd rather believe. It gives me courage and strength that I wouldn't have otherwise.

I've prayed for a miracle, that somehow we'd come up with the right medication or combination thereof that would allow me to live a life I could once only imagine—one in which I'd wake up every day like an average person, without the fear, not only *if*— but *when*—it would be back.

I have, over the years, encountered several uncaring or unsupportive psychiatrists. But take heart.

There are many, many wonderful and caring psychiatrists and psychologists. You may have to do a little searching, but it's worth the time and trouble.

While we were living in Chicago, I was fortunate to find a psychiatrist who was willing to stick by me until we hit upon a combination of medications that have stabilized me for over five years. She is a remarkable, compassionate, and brilliant doctor. She saved my life in more ways than I can ever express and I am forever indebted to her. Even though we no longer live in Chicago, I see her whenever I'm there.

After two or three unsuccessful attempts at finding that kind of commitment from a doctor here in Florida, I have once again found an excellent psychiatrist whom I trust and feel safe with. He has taken over monitoring my medications and has only once had to make an adjustment, which was quite successful.

It has now been over six years since I've had an episode of either depression or hypomania. There are times I'd like to recapture that wonderful hypomanic feeling without the depression that seems to accompany it, but I don't think that's possible; and the ups don't even begin to make up for the horrible lows, believe me.

It hasn't been easy, not only for me, but also for those who have lived through this with me. Imperative to living with and surviving depressive illness is the supportive caring and non-judgmental support of family or friends. In this respect, I have been blessed with an unconditional love from my husband, Michael, his family, my son, Darin, and my closest friend, Laura.

There aren't words to describe how much I am indebted to Michael for his refusal to allow me to give up and for his continuing and enduring love and support.

I hope the sharing of my experience will offer encouragement to those who may now be where I've been. It hasn't been a short or an easy journey, but I believe that I can appreciate, more than the average person, the beauty of a day waking up in a world not distorted by darkness, a world not overwhelmingly oppressive, a world that I thank God for every day, simply because I have survived what once seemed like insurmountable obstacles and arrived at a place that is at long last, a life that holds hope and promise. If it happened for me, I believe it can happen for anyone.

STATISTICS

MAJOR DEPRESSIVE DISORDER

- Is the leading cause of disability in the U.S. for ages 15-44.
- Affects approximately 14.8 million American adults, or about 6.7% of the U.S. population age 18 and older in a given year.
- Is more prevalent in women than men.
- Depression is among the most treatable of psychiatric illnesses. Between 80% and 90% of people with depression respond positively to treatment

BIPOLAR DISORDER

- Affects approximately 5.7 million American adults, or about 2.6% of the U.S. population age 18 and older in a given year.
- Although bipolar disorder is equally common in women and men, research indicates that approximately three times as many women as men experience rapid cycling.
- Bipolar disorder is found in all ages, races, ethnic groups and social classes
- Bipolar disorder is the sixth leading cause of disability in the world.

DYSTHYMIC DISORDER (Chronic, mild depression)
- Symptoms must persist for at least two years in adults (one year in children) to meet criteria for the diagnosis.
- Affects approximately 1.5 percent of the U.S. population

SUICIDE
- Approximately one million people die from suicide every year; one death every 40 seconds
- Mental disorders (particularly depression and substance abuse) are associated with more than 90% of all cases of suicide.

Note: In the U.S. mental disorders are diagnosed based on the Diagnostic and Statistical Manual of Mental Disorders, fourth edition (DSM-IV)

Sources: National Institute of Mental Health, 2007 American Foundation for Suicide Prevention, National Center for Health Statistics, World Health Organization

FLORIDA STATISTICS

According to a recent article in the Florida Times-Union newspaper (September 2, 2007), suicide regularly outpaces homicide. Their source, Florida Vital Statistics, Florida Department of Law Enforcement, shows these statistics from 2005:

Suicide vs. Murder

COUNTY	SUICIDE	MURDER
Florida	2,308	881
Duval County	124	96
Clay County	26	5
St. Johns Co.	21	3
Nassau County	12	0

FAMOUS SHOCK PATIENTS *(website: ect.org)*

Confirmed:
Louis Althusser, French philosopher
Sir Malcolm Arnold, British composer
Antonin Artaud, French playwright and actor
Clara Bow, American actress
Richard Brautigan, American poet
Dick Cavett, American talk show host
Kitty Dukakis, wife of politician Michael Dukakis
Thomas Eagleton, former US Senator from Missouri
Ralph Ellison, American actor
Roky Erickson, American rocker
Frances Farmer, American actress
Janet Frame, New Zealand writer
Connie Francis, American singer
Judy Garland, American actress
Naomi Ginsberg, Allen Ginsburg's mother
Julie Goodyear, British actress
David Helfgott, Australian pianist
Ernest Hemingway, American writer
Vladimir Horowitz, Ukrainian pianist
Pat Ingoldsby, Irish poet
Bob Kaufman, American beat poet
Roland Kohloff, American timpanist
Olga Koklova, Picasso's first wife
Seymour Krim, American author
Vivien Leigh, English actress
Oscar Levant, American pianist and composer

Robert Lowell, American poet
Spike Milligan, British comic
Paul Moravec, American composer
Jennifer O'Neill, American actress
Jimmy Piersall, American baseball player
Robert Pirsig, American author
Sylvia Plath, American poet
Cole Porter, American composer
Dory Previn, American singer/songwriter
Lou Reed, American singer
Paul Robeson, American actor and activist
Michelle Shocked, American singer
Yves Saint-Laurent, French designer
Edie Sedgwick, American actress
Andrew Solomon, American writer
William Styron, American writer
Gene Tierney, American actress
Townes Van Zandt, American songwriter/singer
Rosemarie Von Trapp (mother Maria inspired Sound of Music)
Mark Vonnegut, Kurt Vonnegut's son
John Wieners, American poet
Rose Williams, Tennessee William's sister
Simon Winchester, British writer
Frank Wisner, CIA officer
Stevie Wright, Australian singer
Tammy Wynette, American singer
Last Updated: Apr 15, 2007

REFERENCES

Diagnostic and Statistical Manual of Mental Disorders, 4th ed., text rev. (DSM-IV-TR). American Psychiatric Association 2000.

Touched with Fire: Manic Depressive Illness and the Artistic Temperament by Kay Redfield Jamison, Free Pres, 1996.

An Unquiet Mind: A Memoir of Moods and Madness by Kay Redfield Jamison. Vintage, 1997

Shadowland by William Arnold, published by Berkley, April 1, 1982 Frances Farmer: 1913-1970

National Institute of Mental Health: The Numbers Count. web page: www.nimh

The Bell Jar by Sylvia Plath. Perennial, 2000

Science and Health with Key to the Scriptures by Mary Baker G. Eddy, Christian Science Publishing Society, 1920

The Religion That Kills: Christian Science: Abuse, Neglect, and Mind Control by Linda S. Kramer. Huntington House, 2000

The Noonday Demon: An Atlas of Depression, by
Andrew Soloman. Scribner, 2001

Living Well With Depression and Bipolar Disorder
by John McManamy. HarperCollins, 2006

Undercurrents: A Life Beneath The Surface by
Martha Manning. Harper Collins, 1994

*Shock: The Healing Power of Electroconvulsive
Therapy* by Kitty Dukakis and Larry Tye. Penguin
Group, 2006

Citizens Commission on Human Rights. Website:
www.cchr.org/index.cfm/9162

[1] Diagnostic and Statistical Manual of Mental Disorders, Fourth Edition. Published by the American Psychiaric Association.

[2] National Institute of Mental Health, 2005

[3] *Shadowland* by William Arnold., published by Berkley, April 1, 1982 Frances Farmer: 1913-1970

[4] Citizens Commission on Human Rights:
http://www.cchr.org/index.cfm/9162